5 - 6 - 75

Survival
in the
World
of Work

D. S. Halacy, Jr.

SURVIVAL IN THE WORLD OF WORK

Illustrated with photographs

Charles Scribner's Sons · New York

ACKNOWLEDGMENTS

The Author and the Publisher gratefully acknowledge the following
authors, agents, and publishers for permission to reprint the following
excerpts:

Larry Allen: Excerpt from "A 1972 High School Graduate Looks at
Career Education." From *Essays on Career Education*, ed. by Larry
McClure and Carolyn Brian. Reprinted by permission of Northwest
Regional Educational Laboratory.

Henry Borow: Excerpt from *Man in a World at Work*. Reprinted by
permission of Houghton Mifflin Company.

Jerome Bruner: Excerpt reprinted by permission of the author.

R. G. Collingwood: Excerpt from *An Essay on Philosophic Method*.
Reprinted by permission of the Clarendon Press, Oxford.

James B. Conant: Excerpt reprinted by permission of the author.

Kahlil Gibran: Excerpt from *The Prophet.* Reprinted with permission of the publisher, Alfred A. Knopf, Inc. Copyright 1923 by Kahlil Gibran; renewal copyright 1951 by Administrators C.T.A. of Kahlil Gibran Estate and Mary G. Gibran.

Sidney P. Marland, Jr.: Excerpts reprinted by permission of the author.

Bruce Shertzer: Excerpt from *Career Exploration and Planning.* Reprinted by permission of Houghton Mifflin Company.

James P. Spradley: Excerpt from "Career Education in Cultural Perspective." From *Essays on Career Education,* ed. by Larry McClure and Carolyn Brian. Reprinted by permission of Northwest Regional Educational Laboratory.

George Bernard Shaw: Excerpt from *Man and Superman.* Reprinted by permission of The Society of Authors on behalf of The Bernard Shaw Estate.

Gus Tyler: Excerpts from "Career Education and Society's Imperatives." From *Essays on Career Education,* ed. by Larry McClure and Carolyn Brian. Reprinted by permission of Northwest Regional Educational Laboratory.

ILLUSTRATION ACKNOWLEDGMENTS

The Author and the Publisher gratefully acknowledge the following for permission to reprint photographic material:

American Airlines, 55, 95; American Telephone and Telegraph Company, 37, 69; Fashion Institute of Technology, New York City, 11, 60; High School of the Performing Arts, New York City, —Jerome Eskow, 39, —Martha Swope, 73, 116; The Juilliard School, New York City, 21; New York City Police Department, 91; New York State Department of Health, 18, 44, 64, 98; New York State Department of Labor, 26, 47, 111; United States Department of Labor, 4, 7, 14, 24, 29, 33, 57, 77, 83, 89, 106, 123; United States Lawn Tennis Association, Leon S. Serchuk, 50.

Contents

Survival
in the
World
of Work

WORK IS LOVE MADE VISIBLE
AND IF YOU CANNOT WORK WITH LOVE BUT ONLY
WITH DISTASTE, IT IS BETTER THAT YOU SHOULD LEAVE
YOUR WORK AND SIT AT THE GATE OF THE TEMPLE AND
TAKE ALMS OF THOSE WHO WORK WITH JOY.
FOR IF YOU BAKE BREAD WITH INDIFFERENCE, YOU
BAKE A BITTER BREAD THAT FEEDS BUT HALF MAN'S HUNGER.

Kahlil Gibran
The Prophet

Work: The Joys and the Hang-ups

Webster's first definition of work is: activity in which one exerts strength of faculties to do or perform something: (*a*) sustained physical or mental effort to overcome obstacles and achieve an objective or result; (*b*) the labor, task, or duty that affords one his accustomed means of livelihood.

There are many other definitions of work, of course, and a great variety of opinions of it. Some people even joke about it. English playwright Jerome K. Jerome wrote, "I like work; it fascinates me. I can sit and look at it for hours." And playwright Sir James M. Barrie felt that "Nothing is really work unless you would rather be doing something else."

For many, however, work is anything but a joke. "The

gods hated mankind and condemned them to toil" is an age-old quotation used to establish the eternal, grinding injustice of work. In Genesis 3:19, God tells Adam and Eve: "In the sweat of your face you shall eat bread until you return to the ground." According to some, this was condemnation to a life of slavery. Karl Marx wrote in the *Communist Manifesto:*

> The worker feels himself at home outside his work and feels absent from himself in his work. He feels at home when he is not working, and not at home when he is working. His work is not freely consented to, but is constrained, forced labor. Work is thus not a satisfaction of a need, but only a means to satisfy needs outside work.

English reformers of the nineteenth century protested the plight of children under ten years of age dragging coal cars through the low tunnels of mines. And the "sweatshop" with its child labor persisted in America until fairly recent times. Three decades ago Charlie Chaplin pantomimed a bleak picture of American factory workers in his movie *Modern Times.* Today much is still said and written about the sad condition of the worker: a mere tool in a system that takes advantage of him for its own profit.

NOT ALL THAT BAD

For a number of reasons many of us accept the idea that work is first cousin to a prison sentence, even if the pay is good. Yet it is a fact that some people actually *like* work; they go eagerly to the office, factory, lab, or field and find pleasure in doing a job well and in associating with their fellow workers. George Bernard Shaw wrote of this other side of the coin:

> This is the true joy in life, the being used for a purpose recognized by yourself as a mighty one; the being thoroughly worn out before you are thrown on the scrap heap; the being a force of Nature instead of a feverish, selfish little clod of ailments and grievances complaining that the world will not devote itself to making you happy.

More recently the United Nations Universal Declaration of Human Rights proclaimed that everyone has the *right* to work. And nearly everyone is working! Even for those who are not in love with their jobs, the prospects for an end of work appear to be greatly exaggerated. Although we supposedly are achieving more leisure, statistics refute that belief. Indeed, we seem to be working harder than ever. The work week today is about twenty-five hours shorter than a century ago. Yet nearly one-fifth of today's emancipated employees take a second job, and these "moonlighters" average an *extra* twenty hours of work each week!

Sir Thomas More's "Utopians" worked no more than six hours a day; in Tommaso Campanella's *City of the Sun* the work day was only four hours. Dreams of the easy life have filled our literature for ages, but long ago the poet

Virgil drew an interesting comparison between a world of complete ease and the real one we know. In his *Georgics* he described an earlier world ruled by the god Saturn. So bountiful was this god that people had so little to do they fell deeply asleep. Only when the god Jupiter made life harsh did men rouse from their stupor; necessity stirred them to creative work and great inventions.

Whether or not there is an object lesson for us in this tale, a greater percentage of us work now than in the past. A few decades ago, women made up only a small part of the labor force, yet today they are doing almost half the

work outside the home. In spite of automation that was supposed to make most human work unnecessary, and predictions of the thirty-hour work week, there are more "moonlighters" than ever taking night jobs and weekend jobs in addition to their already full work week.

WHY WE WORK

The increase in work is neither accidental nor incidental. We work to pay for material goods and services for ourselves and our families. Many married women who still do housework and raise the children have taken jobs so the family can have a second car, a motor home, or trips to foreign countries. However, work is not done strictly for economic reasons, although these alone make it inevitable.

The "work ethic," the belief that work is at once a natural right and duty of man, has many names. Because Christians such as Saint Thomas Aquinas and Martin Luther taught that work was the way to serve God, the term *Christian ethic* became popular. This is also called the Protestant ethic, and occasionally the Judeo-Christian ethic.

Faith in the work ethic has prevailed for many centuries and is still a very strong factor in our lives. Psychiatrist Dr. William C. Menninger wrote that work arises from the necessity for self-preservation, the desire to raise a family, and the satisfaction of pleasant relationships with associates on the job. He also suggested that meaningful work provides an outlet for the hostile, aggressive drive which is the major source of creative energy. Dr. Erich Fromm has said that the will to destroy must arise when the will to create cannot be satisfied.

THE GREAT EGO TRIP

Sociologist Abraham Maslow pointed out a hierarchy, or priority list, of human needs:

Physiological needs:
    hunger, thirst
Safety:
    housing, warmth,
    protection from danger
Love:
    companionship, affection
Self-esteem:
    prestige, status
Self-actualization:
    self-expression, creativity

For most of us, work is necessary to satisfy hunger and thirst. Work also provides a roof overhead and the other needs and comforts of life. Marriage and a family require money as well, unless we marry someone with plenty of money. Having taken care of the three most immediate needs, we can satisfy those of self-esteem and self-actualization. And we best experience these as well through rewarding work. In a study of satisfactions achieved and reported by happy workers, these topped the list: recognition, accomplishment, personal growth, responsibility, confidence, status, wealth, security, belonging, and pride. Work, then, is not only necessary for survival but seems to have important rewards on successively higher levels.

Among the clever signs adorning desks and bulletin boards is one that reads: "Time is valuable. Why waste it all working?" Certainly work can be overdone, and Wayne Oates' book *Confessions of a Workaholic* is a light-hearted warning against getting too wrapped up in one's work. At the other extreme is the person who shuns work

completely. For each of us there is an ideal somewhere between the extremes of all work and all play. Surprisingly, that "midpoint" may lie nearer work than play. For example, Dr. Hans Selye, noted authority on stress, points out that he has always worked from four in the morning until six at night. Still working as hard as ever at age sixty-six, and finding it just as rewarding, Selye said, "Short hours are a boon only for those underprivileged who are not good at anything, have no particular taste for anything, and no hunger for achievement. These are the true paupers of mankind."

In Selye's view, looking forward to a time when automation supplants work is "as senseless as looking forward to the day of test-tube babies, making sex superfluous." His comparison of work to sex is interesting, especially when considered with a statement by psychologist Jerome Bruner:

> The neuroses of the young are far more likely to revolve around work than around sex. Therefore, I cannot escape the conclusion that the first order of business in the transformation of our mode of educating is to revolutionize and revivify the idea of vocation or occupation.

THE TROUBLE WITH WORK

Work, like sex, seems to be here to stay and is perhaps almost as vitally necessary. But it is also a fact—and a sad one—that there are millions of people for whom work is grinding, dehumanizing toil which results in the stresses of frustration and even failure. These stresses, Dr. Selye says, in turn produce irreversible *chemical* scars. For such unfortunate people work is a menace to health and life itself.

It is easy to mouth platitudes about work being our greatest blessing, keeping us out of mischief, and being ordained of God, especially if you are the boss. But the work ethic should not be the blind acceptance of pat phrases and the keeping of one's nose to the grindstone. Philosopher George Santayana was more realistic when he wrote, "Certain moralists, without meaning to be satirical, often say that the sovereign cure for unhappiness is work. Unhappily, the work they recommend is better fitted to dull the pain, than to remove its cause." With the same perception, Albert Camus pointed out: "Without work all life goes rotten. But when work is soulless, life stifles and dies."

How much work is soulless is open to question. But the report "Work in America," published in 1973 by the Department of Health, Education, and Welfare, noted that less than half the white-collar workers interviewed said they would choose the same job if they could begin again. Even worse, less than one-fourth of blue-collar workers were happy in *their* jobs! Interestingly, the same report states that almost 80 percent of the college students polled believed that a meaningful career is a very important factor in their lives. The need, apparently, is to see that more of us entering the world of work find our proper place in the vast variety of jobs available.

MISSING THE BUS

Education is our biggest business, and our country currently spends about $100 billion a year for this vital service. It has also been pointed out that 1973 marked a great milestone for our educational system; for the first time more than half the new employees had been trained by educators. Up until that time, the majority had been trained on the job. However, it may be asked how well formal education has done in training people for *rewarding* careers.

In 1971 about 3.7 million young people left school, for one reason or another. Some had successfully completed a useful formal education but many more had not. As a matter of fact, almost 2.5 million left school without skills sufficient for work at a level they should have been capable of. Some left with no salable skills at all. Dropouts totaling about 850,000 left elementary or secondary school during the year. Another 750,000 graduated from high school—with no skills or abilities to offer employers. And 850,000 left college without completing a degree or an organized course leading to a job. All too typical is the complaint of a large utility company that four out of ten applicants lacked the fundamental skills of reading, writing, and arithmetic!

Another problem is that while only one job in seven requires a college or university diploma, most high school students take courses aimed at college—from which many drop out. Although jobs not requiring higher education represent more than 85% of the total available, only a small

fraction of high school students are given training that will qualify them in these fields.

MOTIVATING YOU

Despite discouraging statistics, the world of work is not the dull, chaotic shambles its worst critics say it is. But all is not well either, and such is the nature of our complex society and technology that the situation will get worse unless something is done to help matters. Much has been tried already, and much more will continue to be tried. But in all the efforts to solve the problems of the world of work, it is often forgotten how important the *young person* is in the selection of his or her skill, job, or career and the pursuit of related studies. Certainly many people are interested in the success of the student—parents, teachers, would-be employers, and others. But none can be as personally interested as the student and no one knows the student so well. A former U.S. commissioner of education made this point at the conclusion of a speech on careers: "A young person will grow and flourish increasingly as he becomes *self-motivated* through informed *self-determination* of his own destiny."

No one knows better than you what your interests and abilities are. No one is more keenly interested in your future. And no one can do as good a job of preparing for that future as you can. That is what this book is all about.

THE GREAT LAW OF CULTURE IS: LET EACH BECOME ALL THAT
HE WAS CREATED CAPABLE OF BEING; EXPAND, IF POSSIBLE, TO HIS
FULL GROWTH; RESISTING ALL IMPEDIMENTS, CASTING OFF ALL FOR-
EIGN, ESPECIALLY ALL NOXIOUS ADHESIONS, AND SHOW HIMSELF AT
LENGTH IN HIS OWN SHAPE AND STATURE, BE THESE WHAT THEY
MAY.

Thomas Carlyle
Richter

Doing
Your Thing

Psychologists and sociologists often make comparisons between human behavior and that of animals. Humans are
animals, of course, but with a tremendous difference. Although there are obvious similarities in structure and function between man and some animals, and we are impressed
by the "human" antics of trained monkeys, there is an intellectual gulf between us and the lower animals that these
similarities cannot bridge.

210 MILLION INDIVIDUALS

Animals are much more like each other than men are.
Animals wear no clothes, paint no pictures, and write no

books. One bird differs little from any other bird of the same species and sex. A wild animal lives a life practically identical to that lived a hundred, a thousand, or a million years ago by others of its kind. Not so with humans. Unlike lower animals, which function mostly with built-in knowledge that enables many of them to survive on their own at a tender age (sometimes right from birth), humans come in much greater variety and are far more capable of developing different potentials. Humans are not peas in a pod, they are individuals.

A great variety of lifestyles exists because different people want different things. Despite outward similarities, and the fact that internal structure is pretty much a standard design of plumbing and structural members, individual intellectual and emotional makeups are very different. If this were not so, there would be no authors or readers, no doctors or dentists, aeronautical engineers or ballet dancers. We would all be much alike, just as lions are much alike. Life would be very simple and also very dull, although we would not realize it was dull. We would live each day like other days, with little thought of yesterday or last week, and not even a concept of tomorrow.

Instead of being merely an organ that responds to outside stimuli, the human mind is a motivating force in its own right. Not the servant of muscles, nerves, blood, and flesh responding to environment, but the *master;* with the survival and emotional systems of the body responding to it. Unlike lower animals, which mostly *react* to the environment, humans have the ability and the need to *act* of themselves. We humans, then, have minds that are light-years ahead of animal minds. We are also vastly different from each other. (Even "identical" twins, genetically as similar as humans can be, are not truly identical.) If we *were* all the same we might get along better with one another, but along with the problems we have as human beings there are also great challenges and potential rewards.

ROLES AND GOALS

The purpose of a wild animal in life is as obvious as it is simple: to get through today with a full stomach and to repeat such success tomorrow, and the next day, until life has run its course. Humans, on the other hand, want life to be meaningful, stimulating, and rewarding. Our brains are often described as problem-solving machines, and life is the biggest of our problems, especially if our goal is to make it as rich and full as possible.

Each of us has a purpose, a role it is important to fill. For a writer it is communicating thoughts to others. For some people writing is far less important than building a bridge. Or teaching a class of sixth graders, or developing an engine that is twice as efficient as anything now running and won't pollute the atmosphere with smoke and noise. There is a story about a farmer who had struggled all his life on a failing farm. A friend asked him what he would do if some rich relative left him a million dollars. "I reckon I'd just farm till the money ran out!" he responded. Unlike the farmers of prehistory, who tilled the soil only for sustenance, this man farmed because it was a challenge he had to meet against all odds.

It has been correctly said that life is not a harbor or a destination, but only the long journey to such a place. Happy are those who like to travel, and enjoy the trip! And miserable the person working below decks on life's ocean liner simply to reach old age with enough saved to pay the undertaker.

ONE-THIRD OF YOUR LIFE

Tragically, millions of people spend eight or more hours a day on a job and hate every hour, just living for the time when they can escape from their prison. They then proceed to dull their minds with television, strong drink or drugs, and other diversions. It is fine to do your thing after work. But beware the danger in doing it just in retaliation against a demoralizing job.

Often the person who has had it up to here at work is unable to relax during off hours. He has fought with his work, his boss, and his fellow workers for eight hours. He is worrying about switching to another job, or, worse yet, getting fired from this one before he finds a better one. Because he does not like his work—and in fact may actively hate it!—his pay may not advance as fast as the cost-of-living index does. As a result of all this, the jobholder takes to growling at his wife when he gets home from work. His wife snaps at the children, who pass the punishment down the line until the smallest one kicks the dog, who in turn chases the cat up the tree. And the breadwinner's ulcer requires large doses of bicarbonate of soda.

To make his plight worse, there is that sickening character down the block who bubbles over about his *stimulating* job—in the same office! This oddball goes fishing because he enjoys fishing, and not just to forget the miseries of a nine-to-five stint at work.

How much better to work at something you like to do and can do well. Something in which you will be more successful and happy, and probably make more money—if money is important to you. Nor is this such an unattainable goal. For each job a person might despise, there is another—or a dozen—in which he could do well. Far from condemning us to a lifetime of slave-like labor, civilization offers us a choice of work to meet our variety of interests and aptitudes.

DOING YOUR OWN THING

In ancient times, when nearly everyone tilled the soil, we were all in it together. Cutting grain was not especially

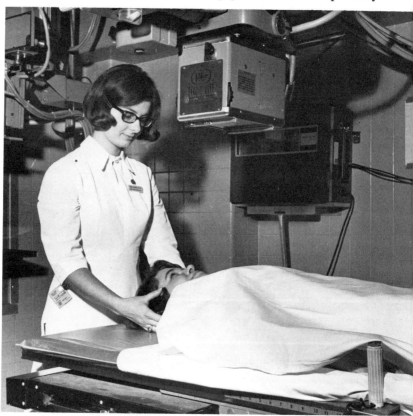

stimulating but what else was a person to do? The need to eat made the job, as well as the food, more palatable. Today the situation is far different, for there are dozens of basically different jobs, and thousands of further divisions of specialization. There is also unemployment, underemployment, and overemployment. There is overtime, but there are cutbacks and layoffs as well. Yet, in spite of all the problems of work today, how much better the situation than in ancient times. No longer must round pegs go into square holes, as they did when everyone farmed or hunted for a living. With their individuality, different interests, and different abilities, humans have created a work world with room in it for all types of people.

The happiest people in the world are those who work at something they like, whose vocation is their avocation as well. The expression "I love my job" may have a strange ring, but lucky is the worker who can truthfully make that statement—not just on payday but every day of the week including Friday. I fly a sailplane just for the fun of it. Yet I know men who earn their living doing that. I also enjoy building model aircraft as a hobby and envy those who can work at this for pay. Once I built real aircraft for a living and the difference between that and my previous job of installing furnaces was the difference between day and night, enjoyment and drudgery.

All of us are trying to express ourselves, but too often we cut off that inner voice and listen instead to the advice of "experts" to get into this or that line of work. "There's always a need there," they say. "Anyone can do *anything*" is more such advice. "All you have to do is put your heart into it.'' Most teachers probably could be taught to install bathtubs, and most plumbers probably could be put through four years of education courses and certified as teachers. It is even possible that some of these changes *should* take place. But the sad truth is that many have been sidetracked from a career in the building trades to teaching. And many a potentially good teacher has turned computer programmer (or better yet, computer analyst) because "they" say that's where the action, the prestige, and the money are.

It would be ridiculous to suggest that a person is better off playing marbles all his life, or painting horrible watercolors, just because these things turn him or her on. And it would be hard to survive economically by lying under a tree and staring at the sky. But a person who loves books might be happier working in a book store, or sitting at a typewriter writing books, than programming a computer or working as a marine biologist, no matter how "in" the latter vocations are.

What *is* your thing? Some of us are interested in government, others in military tasks. Some prefer to be on their own, others would rather work in a group. You probably already have a good idea of your own likes and dislikes, your abilities and shortcomings. Happily, we generally do best what we like best. Few musicians hate music, few politicians detest dealing with people, few storekeepers dislike serving the public. All of which suggests that doing your own thing is a sensible approach to a lifetime of work.

If you love basketball and get a kick out of coaching younger boys and girls in this sport, you have a clue. If you love sketching and fashions, your destiny may be in advertising art, if you are good enough. If you know the difference between mathematics and arithmetic, and can't get enough of the former, you may do better as a mathematician than as a real estate salesman, even though your dad has made a fortune selling homes and is begging you to carry on the family business.

Most of us do not realize the exciting scope of the world of work. Indeed, it is difficult for anyone to believe that there can really be thousands of different jobs. But our society has created this broad spectrum of vocations and we are shortsighted if we do not take advantage of the opportunities. The first steps toward this goal are to investigate the world of work and to explore the possibilities that appeal to you.

The World of Work

There was a time when all humans had but one occupation. It was called "staying alive" and it generally took up most of the day, every day. There are still such primitive groups of people in the world and from time to time these "Stone Age" tribes make the headlines. But because we demand more than just survival, and continually seek new achievements, we produced civilization. This more complex lifestyle could originate only in places where there were ample natural resources and a favorable environment. Under these conditions, the population increased and there came a breathing spell in the process of survival. There was time to relax and think, and man had a mind for thinking. Egyptian officials wrote of "vocational guidance" 4,500 years ago, and in his *Republic,* Plato urged a division of labor based on the different talents of mankind.

It was obvious early in human existence that there were needs other than just those of the flesh. The saying that man does not live by bread alone implies intellectual and spiritual needs too. Painting, drawing, engraving, modeling, sculpting, architecture, and literature are examples of these. Music too fills a deep, instinctive need. Another, strangely pressing, need has always been for an understanding of man's origin and destiny. Religion slowly emerged.

In time, the primitive clan chief became a king with military leaders to spread his empire. Here was a further division of labor, with new opportunities in the choice of work. While an army of soldiers waged war on enemies, another army of clerks and scribes kept track of the booty. They also taxed the king's subjects to pay for his castle, soldiers, roads, and other public works. We think we pay crushing taxes today, but many ancient civilizations were ruined by the grandiose projects of their kings. The great temples of Asia are examples of such projects as are the pyramids and sphinxes in Egypt, the marvelous roads of the Persians and the Romans, and the spectacular sacrificial temples of the Incas in the New World.

INDUSTRIAL REVOLUTION

The agricultural revolution had created a complex work world; the coming of mechanized industry greatly broadened the trend. At first power had to come from living machines—animals or men. Sometimes the manpower was that of slaves, a commodity to be bought and sold. When waterwheels and windmills began to supplement the power of muscles, new vocations emerged. Vehicles created jobs for the "wheelwright" and "wainright," or wagon builder. Steam engines and internal-combustion engines hastened the process, creating a need for engineers and designers, metal workers to build the engines, and mechanics to tend and repair them.

To fuel the new engines, coal mining boomed, and so did the production of oil and gas. Once men had walked,

or ridden animals; with powered vehicles they crossed continents, sailed the oceans and rivers, and flew through the air. Transportation became one of our biggest industries. Trade, exploration, and technology led to increased industrial efficiency, growth of population, and further expansion of civilization. In industrialized countries one farmer fed dozens of people instead of one, and those dozens had to do something else if they wanted to eat the food the farmer raised. (Unless they bought his produce the farmer himself would come on hard times—although at least he would have something to eat.)

It was Aristotle who wrote, "If every instrument could do its own work, if the shuttle could weave, and the plectrum pluck the lyre without a guiding hand, foremen would not need workers, nor masters, slaves." Aristotle was a wise man, but this dream of his has yet to come true. One of the most remarkable things about work is that such a great part of the population is involved in it. It would seem that as industry and agriculture became more efficient and productive there would be *less* need for workers. Indeed, there were cries of alarm from telephone workers' unions when automatic switching equipment was installed. Automation, it was feared, would mean the loss of countless jobs as the "old-fashioned" human operator was replaced by electrical switches. Yet the telephone companies now employ more people than before, including many switchboard operators. Computers were also considered a menace to those who handled paperwork before the electronic machines were developed, yet there seem to be more clerical workers needed all the time. In early times few women worked outside the home. But if all working women left their jobs today, many goods and services would be unavailable, for women now make up almost half our work force!

THE MALE MYTH

Gus Tyler, assistant president of the International Garment Workers Union and responsible for its departments of education, politics, and training, has commented interestingly on what he calls the "male myth":

The male myth holds that the world of work is no world for women. Hence, with some exceptions, vocational (career) education is male oriented. The fact is, women have moved into the labor force so rapidly

that within a few years females will represent 50 percent of the employed. At present they compose about 40 percent. In 1950 they were only 30 percent. In 1948 only 18 percent of the mothers held jobs away from home; by 1970 the percent had risen to 43. Of mothers with children between 6 and 17, half work; of those with children under 6, one-third work; with children under 3, one-quarter work. The trend is likely to be accelerated because (*a*) the service economy provides more opportunities for light neighborhood-based parttime work; (*b*) because women's lib will open greater opportunities in the professions; and (*c*) because the pressures of our times drive wives and mothers to work to pay for the mortgage on a home in a better neighborhood and for college tuition for the kids.

A POST-INDUSTRIAL SOCIETY

We are now on the threshold of what some analysts call the "post-industrial" society, a term that needs clarification. We seldom speak of the "post-agricultural" society, for we still must have food and drink, of course. The industrial society put the majority of our people into the production of material goods rather than food. Homes, manufacture of automobiles, appliances, sporting goods, and such things took most of our effort. Now most of our work effort is going into the "service industries." Education is an example of a service. So are tourism, entertainment, medicine, counseling, and so on. The post-industrial society, in which we devote more of our energy to providing each other with services rather than food or material goods, is possible because of the productivity and efficiency of both agriculture and industry.

30,000 DIFFERENT JOBS

Basically there are three broad categories of employment: agriculture, manufacturing, and the service industries. However, there are thousands of different jobs, careers, professions, or positions. We should realize that these cut across the basic categories. For example, scientists are involved in all three as are bookkeepers, salesmen, and mechanics. There is something, or several things, suited to nearly everyone looking for work.

Years ago, English political scientist C. Northcote Parkinson formulated "Parkinson's Law," which says that any venture tends to grow and make an empire of itself. Actually, this law seems to have been in operation almost from the beginning of civilized life, for the human mind bulges with plans and projects that expand to occupy all available space and time. Our fertile imaginations constantly dream up new ways to embellish and complicate life. It is said that many centuries have passed since any one scientist could comprehend *all* of science. Today science has become even more specialized and scientists are no longer merely physicists or astronomers. Within these already specialized sciences, there are further breakdowns into nuclear physics (with further subdisciplines), molecular physics, astrophysics, radio astronomy, and so on *ad infinitum*. A listing of scientific disciplines ranges from acoustics to zymurgy (a branch of the chemistry of fermentation), with thousands of fields in between. Science, of course, is but one small part of all the divisions of labor, and relatively few people are employed as scientists.

While estimates of different job classifications range as high as 30,000, no one knows for sure exactly how many

there are (perhaps one job classification is that of trying to find out!). Of course all these classifications are not uniquely different from one another, nor is a person suited to only one particular job. There is much overlap, and the career education concept—to be considered in Chapter 7—breaks the thousands of classifications down into fifteen "clusters" for easier exploration of the world of work:

Communication and Media
Health
Marine Science
Agri-business and Natural Resources
Hospitality and Recreation
Transportation
Public Service
Personal Services
Fine Arts and Humanities
Business and Office
Manufacturing
Consumer and Homemaking Education
Environment
Construction
Marketing and Distribution

It is interesting to note that of these fifteen clusters only one can be positively identified as agriculture. Perhaps five qualify as manufacturing. Thus nine are service related; evidence of how the agricultural society has given way to the industrial and finally the post-industrial.

An obvious way of considering jobs is by industry. Some of us are interested in aviation, some in road building. Electronics or chemical engineering appeal to others. There are newer fields with great appeal, such as pollution abatement, noise control, speech therapy, and so on. Education is vast in scope, as are government work and labor relations. Office work appeals to some; others would feel imprisoned if they could not work in the open. Job opportunities and careers depend on one's abilities, geographic location, choice of lifestyle, and other factors.

In the world of work some individuals are "thinkers" and some are "doers." Research scientists, philosophers, psychologists, some medical men, government analysts, and others work principally with their minds. They do not produce "hardware," but ideas and directions for others to put into practice. Doers are of many kinds. Despite industrialization, mechanization, and computerized automation, some work is still done much as it always has been, by using one's hands to dig a ditch, nail boards together, or mortar bricks into a wall. Some doers use machines; for example, a factory worker operates a traveling crane to carry large tanks from one assembly area to another, a car painter uses a spray gun, welders work with flaming gas torches that fuse metals together.

Are you content to take instruction, or do you want to be in charge of a group? Do you prefer to work with others, or by yourself? Meeting the public is a job that provides not only an income but great personal satisfaction to many who would be miserable operating a drill press or shoeing horses.

Thus far we have been talking about the "horizontal" range of careers, sweeping across a number of different fields of work. Within each field itself there is also a great "vertical" range. You may be interested in medicine at a number of different levels: as a dental hygienist, or as a researcher seeking a cure for cancer; a family doctor in a small town, or a heart specialist in a skyscraper hospital serving a city of two million; a nurse or laboratory technician. Too often this vertical range of opportunities and responsibilities is not fully appreciated.

Different jobs and professions have different financial rewards. There are considerations besides money, surely, and many young people today seem particularly concerned with these other values. A missionary in a foreign land is generally poor in pocket but can be wealthy in spirit and fulfillment. For some, the life of a cowboy in a remote line shack, or a ranger manning a fire lookout, cannot be matched. For others, both tasks would be boring.

SURVEYING THE WORLD OF WORK

If you already know about all the jobs available you are probably not much in need of this chapter. But if you are hazy about the opportunities that exist besides teaching, computer programming, marine biology, and space science, for example, a bit of research is in order. Look at the section of the newspaper devoted to "Help Wanted" advertisements. In most large cities, this fills several pages and includes a great variety of positions. They will give you an idea of what is available. Look around you too.

The building trades offer many jobs, including plumbing, carpentry, masonry, electrical work, roofing, painting, cement finishing, truck driving, drafting, and architecture. Think about that office building downtown. In it are janitors, elevator operators (if the computer hasn't taken over that job yet!), food handlers, office managers, secretaries, stenographers, computer personnel, salesmen, file clerks, typists. Your city provides many services: police and fire protection, inspections of various kinds, appraisals, road building, maintenance work, water service, garbage collection, and construction planning.

Your school should be a help to you in exploring the world of work. Representatives of business and industry give talks describing their job opportunities, and often

field trips are planned for on-the-spot visits. The state employment office should be able to provide information on the scope and availability of jobs in your area. The main thing is to get your survey done. If you don't know what is out there, your chances of finding the right job are slim indeed.

THE COLOR OF YOUR COLLAR

We have noted that one job in seven in our country requires college or university training for four years or more. If you plan to be a doctor or veterinarian, engineer, astronomer, chemist, or teacher, in most cases you are committing yourself for four to eight years and more of study. If you are that one in seven you have your work cut out for you, and at the end of that long, hard road a meaningful profession awaits you. But if you don't see such a future for yourself there is still plenty of opportunity for the other six out of seven.

For a long time, vocational education and a job in the manual trades or similar employment areas was considered the fate of someone not capable of making it as a professional. Such workers were modestly paid, had few fringe benefits, and little protection against layoffs. The picture has changed so greatly in recent years that plumbers and truck drivers earn as much and often more than teachers and engineers. There is certainly no disgrace in a skilled trade that pays $20,000 a year for a four-day week, plus benefits including vacation, insurance, credit union, and so on! The blue-collar field is enjoying great popularity as its workers begin to outdo white-collar types who historically have earned more pay and prestige.

In 1900 37 percent of American workers were farmers; today only 6 percent do such work. Blue-collar workers have remained almost exactly the same percentage of the work force since 1900, and today represent 37 percent of the working population. White-collar workers, on the other hand, have risen from 18 to 44 percent. The fastest growing of these are professionals and technical workers, who have actually tripled their share of jobs. Interestingly, the once clear distinctions between so-called white-collar and blue-collar workers are beginning to blur. Equality of pay helps to wipe out former differences, and so does the constant upgrading of mechanical and technical work. Socially too the old separations are fading.

There is also a continuing trend away from self-employment. In 1940 about one person in five worked for himself; the figure is now only one in seven. The size of businesses has increased too, so that most people work for firms employing large numbers. Understandably, many young people do not look forward to factory work, or to being a computerized payroll card in a huge, impersonal company.

WORKING HARD AND WORKING EASY

The grinding drudgery of some kinds of work is what the poet William Blake was attacking when he wrote of England's "dark Satanic mills," and surely we would not want to work under such conditions. In a complex society such as ours it is very easy to lose sight of what is going on, to find no meaning in our drab occupation of riveting widget A onto plate B or filing folders under A to Z. However, although it is often said that the dehumanization of the factory is still with us today, the report "Work in America," prepared by the Department of Health, Education, and Welfare, points out that less than 2 percent of our work force toil on assembly lines. And while for some there is still the monotonous routine of repetitive tasks, conditions are certainly better than those endured in the sweatshops of olden times.

How hard or how easy *do* you want your vocational life to be? In earlier times a town might offer only a half-dozen varieties of shop work, a few low-paying teaching jobs, and the standard five-and-a-half-day week at the factory. If a man was willing to work at night his check would be a few dollars more a week. If he didn't like the employment choices he could leave town, or go hungry. Today a much greater range of employment is available. With the variety of jobs, shifts, part-time opportunities, and so on, you can achieve a lifestyle more suited to your wishes.

It is possible to earn several hundred dollars a week and end the year with only a few of them in the bank. It is also possible to live on less than a hundred dollars a week and enjoy life more than the person who scrambles so hard for his big salary—a big chunk of which goes to an army of tax collectors.

For some people, status and prestige are all-important; they must live on the grand scale even if it means borrowing to the limit and sometimes racing their checks to the bank. Other people seem as happy on a fraction as much money—like the widowed secretary I knew whose income was just slightly above what the government considered the poverty level. With modest tastes and common sense in spending, she maintained a small but comfortable home, a car, and color television, and could afford recreation,

including bowling, and little league baseball in season for her three boys.

In today's world you can work as hard as you like, or almost as easy as you like, realizing that it does require a certain minimum number of dollars to keep body and soul together, and both the wolf and the bill collector away from the door.

WHY WE WORK

Some dreamers predict a day when all work will be done by machines, and man himself will be free to do whatever he likes. Such a situation will probably not come in our time, particularly when a greater percentage of us are working now than ever before. Such diligence is based on our deep-rooted needs. Quite obviously, we work to enjoy food, shelter, transportation, and all the goods and services we have become accustomed to. It would be difficult or impossible for any individual to build a home, car, radio, and television set, educate children, raise food, print reading material, provide entertainment, build recreational facilities, fight wars, run the city, the state, and the federal government, take care of the sick and needy, dam the rivers, deliver the mail, maintain the roads, fly the airplanes, and run the trains. Instead, each of us pays for these many goods and services with our own work of a specialized nature.

It is often suggested that our only hope is to return to the simple life. There is a great appeal in this idea, because of pollution, traffic jams, murder in the streets, high prices,

indifferent workmanship, and the often cold and impersonal life of the big city. Unfortunately, however, the return to the idyllic life the poets sing about is more difficult than it might seem and few are willing to take the first backward step.

When Columbus blundered onto the New World, the "natural food chain" in North America supported about one million Indians. "Going back to nature" now would mean that fewer than that number of us could exist—and the word is well chosen—in the United States. We could survive without central heating and refrigeration, fast cars, color television, and amplified rock. But most of us would find it very difficult to live in ways even our grandparents have forgotten. In all the glowing praise for the good old days there is surprisingly little mention of the dirt, disease, poverty, slavery, danger, starvation, and other bad features of early life.

Our society seems to have reached a point of no return; we have burned our natural bridges behind us. Going back to the life of those who pioneered our country would eliminate all but a handful of us so that primitive food-gathering, farming, and hunting could once more be practiced. The better solution is to find how we as individuals best fit into the world of work that makes modern living possible. Those who really want the rugged, old-fashioned life can achieve it. There are still working cowboys, and roving "farriers" to shoe their horses. Some people are happy tending small farms in remote areas where taxes are low and there are no rent payments or utility bills. A few hours of extra labor once in a while provides enough money to buy the necessities that can't be grown. It is also possible to be happy in the urban environment that the great majority of Americans live in. Many workers *are* happy, and many more could be—if they would think carefully and seriously before locking themselves into the world of work in a way that can bring dissatisfaction, and even misery.

Where YOU Belong

With the vast variety of work available it is difficult to understand why so many of us don't find our proper place in the scheme of things. Ironically, it may be that the wide choice itself confuses us and helps put us in a job we not only don't fit but may soon learn to hate. Psychiatrists do a thriving business, at rates of $50 and more an hour, and many of their patients are employees improperly matched to their jobs. The "ulcer route" is no joke for those beset by pressures and frustrations beyond their ability to bear. Equally great frustrations can come from the reverse situation—that of the worker who is *under*employed and unfulfilled.

Einstein adding columns of numbers for a living or Picasso painting flowers on mass-produced pottery would be classic examples of underemployment. Most work problems are not so flagrant. However, the young person who should be selling real estate but caved in to parental pressures to manage the family mortuary suffers too. Even more important than your effort on the job is your effort in selecting that job in the first place. Doing your thing is important in seeking the pleasures of life. In the world of work you can do your own thing and be paid well for it; usually more than for something that isn't your cup of tea.

A word of caution is in order. There are many young people who can skillfully paint houses, or make plumbing repairs, and yet should not get into these as a life work. Maybe your dad is a master painter and has insisted you work for him weekends and summers. It pays well and offers steady employment. But swinging a brush and splashing a roller doesn't grab you all that much. You may not actively despise the life of a painter, but you have no love for it either. Working a few hours a week at a money-making chore is one thing, committing oneself for life is a much more serious business. Just because you *can* do something doesn't always mean you *should* do it for a living, unless there is nothing else you like better.

THAT LITTLE OLD DECISION-MAKER: YOU

Once people thought that kings ruled by divine right, and that the son of a king was naturally destined to rule in his turn. Shakespeare and his contemporaries called this the "natural chain of being," and it had a nice ring, particularly to those who were running things. Despite some pretty obvious evidence to the contrary, it was argued that "blood would tell." The king would produce future kings, and warriors more fighting men. Just as the young prince was expected to step up to the throne, and generally did, the carpenter's son became a carpenter; the scribe brought his boy up to read and write. A man's calling was often spelled out in the letters of his family name: Cartwright, Miller, or Baker.

It is true that there is often a striking similarity between father and son, or mother and daughter. But now that we know more about genetics we understand why some noble kings sired drunkards, and the town drunk now and again fathered a mathematical wizard, or a great painter. For Junior may be the "spittin' image" of Dad in every respect, or he may be a throwback to Grandpa Smart (or Dull) on Mother's side of the family. He may even be just himself, with little resemblance to anyone in the family.

Even before scientists learned about genes, society changed to make more opportunity for the variety of offspring in a family. The European custom of "primogeniture" gave the family estate to the eldest son, who would be something of a lamebrain if he didn't take it, even if running a castle wasn't his first choice, or tending a draper's shop gave him the fidgets. It was a tidy living, and who could fight custom? But America discarded the idea of primogeniture, letting all the children share alike in an estate. Thus family businesses were more likely to break up and leave the young people free to pursue another field with their legacy. Uncle Sam's Internal Revenuers

have done their bit too in this respect. Estate taxes sometimes wipe out the family business so a son can't follow in
his father's footsteps even if he wants to manufacture
widgets.

As a result, ancient guidelines and traditions don't hold
so fast anymore. There are still countries where Mom and
Dad decide whom daughter will marry, sometimes sealing
the bargain while she is still a child. This seldom happens
in our country now, but quite often parents try to influence
what Janie will be when she grows up. Most parents are
naturally and sincerely concerned about the future of their
children and should get credit for that concern. But wise
parents realize that much as they'd like Janie to go to the
same college or university and aim at the same career as

her mother, her talents may lie elsewhere. Maybe the reason that she *wants* to be different is because she *is* different.

A lot of people are going to try to decide where you will spend your working days. Your parents have already given the matter much thought and passed on some of these thoughts to you. So have other relatives. Your teachers, your counselors, maybe your minister, Scout leader, coach, neighbors, local businessmen, and a host of others also get into the act. How active have *you* been, and will you be, in picking your work? Are you wishy-washy enough to grab the first suggestion from family, friends, or educators? This easy approach might do, but it might also be the great tragedy of your life.

Even worse is the plight of the guy or gal who hasn't given the job matter any thought at all. Life is full and beautiful at the moment with social affairs, music, sports, and the like. The sun comes up each day and there is plenty of food on the table. Lots of jobs are available and recruiters will most likely entice you off to IBM at a five-figure salary as some sort of way-out computer type. They may—but they probably won't. And you'll get right down to the wire, and then have to decide in a few short months something you should have been planning for years. If you haven't been thinking seriously about your future, start now.

A VERY PERSONAL MATTER

Different people belong in different jobs, so it is well to consider our many personal differences. One such difference separates the boys from the girls. There are still barriers for both sexes to some jobs. Most plumbers are men; most nurses are women. But this basic difference is slowly becoming less troublesome. Today we see women telephone linemen and auto shop mechanics, women in the military, and women as jockeys at the race track.

Men and women are different. But so are men different from other men, and women from other women. It is these differences in the total makeup we call personality that are so important to us—and to society—in the selection of our work. The ancient Greeks attempted to classify different personality types according to a system of "humors." Until fairly recently people were often categorized as "sanguine," "choleric," "phlegmatic," or "melancholic," according to the suspected predominance of certain body juices. Psychiatrist Carl Gustav Jung pointed out the differences in "introverted" and "extroverted" people. And long ago an educator attempted to extend the now discredited "science" of phrenology (reading bumps on the head to find personality traits) to something he called "vocophy," or the planning of one's vocation from the shape of one's head!

As yet, we do not have infallible rules for pinning down personality. But most agree that there are personality traits, and that they probably have a bearing on how well or how poorly we will do in various endeavors. Then there is the matter of intelligence. A single IQ score is obviously not all that is involved; there are also many skills and abilities we possess on an individual basis. We have differing interests too, and varied drives and motivations. Because

of these factors, not all of us are suited to be farmers, or airline pilots, or dental surgeons. Which is fortunate, because we couldn't all work at these things.

GETTING IT ALL TOGETHER

How should people and jobs be matched up? One approach would be for someone in authority to survey the needs of society and then simply draft people to do the work. In times past kings or their agents did this, conscripting the handiest five hundred subjects into the army, the road gang, or as galley slaves to row warships up and down the Mediterranean. Sailors were "shanghaied" onto ships against their will. The draft until recently put many into the military service whether they wanted to go or not. These are effective means of filling jobs, but only at a high cost for those whose freedom is sacrificed.

Another selection method would be for job seekers to survey the available jobs and then attempt to fit themselves into what each thought was the best for him or her. But why not survey yourself first, and *then* look at the jobs? Long before you were aware of the world of work you were aware of yourself. You should be more concerned with your personality as a beginning point for job selection.

Don't make the mistake of thinking that the working third of your time is separated cleanly from the other two-thirds. Rare is the person who can completely compartmentalize his life; most of us find great overlapping of our jobs and the rest of our lives. This includes social life, leisure, and friends and acquaintances. In short, our work affects our whole way of life. Professor James P. Spradley, a writer on urban affairs, puts it this way:

> Students must learn about the occupational cultures they will be part of for any particular career. The world of work is not merely forty hours a week, income and promotions. It is a lifestyle, a set of values and assumptions. It means membership in a group

with its own customs and mores. The satisfactions and frustrations of a career are results of this wider occupational culture far more than they are dependent on the income and status of the job.

Consider this evaluation carefully. Had you realized that there is an "occupational culture," or that your lifestyle would be largely determined by your work? "It's only a job" is a very shortsighted way of looking at the situation. For finding your proper place in the world of work is to a large extent finding yourself. Give the search the consideration it deserves!

AIMING HIGH

There is a lesson that golfers have to learn about putting: It is better to putt a foot past the hole than a foot short. The reason is simply that if you are long you may miss, but there is also a chance that you may sink the putt. If you are short you are definitely not going to make it. Consider this in choosing your career.

Standard advice is to "begin at the beginning," "start small," "take one step at a time," "learn to walk before you run," *ad infinitum,* and *ad nauseum.* But there's a lesson skiers finally must learn on steep slopes. At some point you have to push off straight down a hill so steep it seems you'll fall over the points of your skis and not hit anything until you reach the bottom of Suicide Run. But after a few such breathtaking tries, you are skiing like Jean-Claude Killy—or so it seems.

There was once a man who had admired a girl from a distance for a long time. She was undoubtedly the most beautiful girl in all the world. More than anything he longed to ask her for a date, but he kept putting it off because he knew he had no chance. However, there came a day when he could resist no longer. He asked her to go out with him, and then braced himself for her refusal. Instead, her face lighted up with something strangely like relief. "I thought you were never going to ask me!" she

said. Which may be the case with that dream job you
heard about, but fear you don't have the credentials for.
About the worst a prospective boss can do is to say no,
and that only hurts for a little while.

Faint heart never won fair lady, and that includes the
Goddess of Success. You want to get that sports counselor
job at summer camp but there are half-a-dozen others better than you? Maybe the person doing the hiring doesn't
know that. Or has to sign someone up fast to meet the
schedule. Or the six others have better jobs, or don't plan
to work this summer. And if someone who is not even as
good as you lands the job, where are you for being so
cautious? Let your career-planning motto be to aim high.
And if you don't lower your sights until you have to, you
may not have to.

THE TRUE TEST OF A CIVILIZATION IS NOT THE
CENSUS, NOR THE SIZE OF CITIES, NOR THE CROPS—
NO, BUT THE KIND OF MAN THE COUNTRY TURNS OUT.

Ralph Waldo Emerson
Society and Solitude

Testing:
1, 2, 3

We have noted that most people have obvious interests and abilities which are at least a hint of the vocational field that will best reward their talents. Fortunately there are ways of finding more specific guidelines toward the right job for you. By now you may be weary and wary of tests but there are certain kinds you might very profitably consider.

If you could live for hundreds of years, you could try out a great number of jobs and find one exactly right for you. But there are no more Methuselahs, and such a slow process would not be very practical for finding your place anyway. Testing, properly used, explores ahead of time your various interests and abilities to learn the sort of work you like, are suited to, and can succeed in. For years such testing was used quite generally but in recent times it has come under fire. As with most arguments, there is much to be said on each side.

Have you ever done a sorting job like separating the good apples from the bad, small ears of corn from the larger, or chipped marbles from the perfect ones? There is understandable resistance to the idea of "grading" people as we do corn, or measuring human ability like the electrical characteristics of a transistor. We don't sort and match humans to jobs in such a mechanical way, but it is possible to do some useful evaluating in advance. For example, whether or not a person can stand up under the strain of driving a city bus through rush-hour traffic, making change with difficult passengers, and worrying about traffic policemen all the while. Or if one could do scientific research that requires long hours working alone.

THE REASONS FOR TESTING

If you've ever had to sort potatoes, you probably thought of a simpler test for finding the bad ones: Cook them *all,* and just don't eat those that are obviously spoiled. You can do the same kind of testing with a car or airplane. Start out on a cross-country trip with no mechanical inspection or checkup. If you reach your destination, obviously everything was okay and you wasted no valuable time or money on tests. If you broke down somewhere along the way, you gained valuable information too: there *was* something wrong, and you found it out. If you were flying, of course, the results might be embarrassing or even fatal.

There is a need for testing, including the testing of people. A bank manager would rather not have a teller who can't do arithmetic and who can't meet people cheerfully. If he can also avoid those who might be tempted to help themselves to cash bonuses, so much the better. So, before getting a job in a bank one generally must pass a battery of tests.

Occasionally we get a bad potato or a bad egg from the store. And occasionally the bank gets a bad egg back of the teller's window too. Testing is not perfect; it can fail in two ways. It may not screen out all the green apples, or it may erroneously screen out some that are ripe. You may remember times when you failed a test on material you thought you knew well. And maybe you squeaked by on another test that time you went to a rock concert instead of studying. However, we don't expect a pitcher to win all his games, although this would delight his manager. If the pitcher wins more than half, he stays on the team; because in the long run a team wins pennants that way. Testing is likewise a statistical process. Some undersize widgets may get through, and some good ones may be thrown out in the screening process. But *most* of the bad ones won't get through. And *most* of the good ones will make it.

We are being tested more often than we realize. When you go out on a date you are being tested. If you or your date doesn't pass the test, you don't go out with that particular individual again. If you apply for a job as bouncer and the club owner estimates your weight at about 120 pounds soaking wet, you'll flunk that test too. Write a job application for a firm that publishes encyclopedias and misspell the words "dear," "salary," and "encyclopedia," and there will be no job for you, unless it's a comic dictionary they have in mind.

If there were no way to test, the world would be in a confused state. Gravity keeps our feet on the ground, it tells us which way is up. In a rational world it is possible to test things to see if they "make the grade." We can inspect a new car to see if it meets government pollution standards, or a new drug to see if it is free from cancer-inducing agents. Of course, a test must fit the application. A businessman might hire a clerk who "looks capable" but find over the following weeks that the new employee cannot type, spell, file, or even make a good cup of coffee. So he gives a spelling test and a few other basics to the next applicant.

Testing is simply a way of learning ahead of time whether or not a prospective employee has the necessary abilities to make money for an employer. Everyone should be interested in that aspect, because when the total system works well, it benefits all of us. But as individuals we have a much bigger personal stake in our job. If we buy a home nearby and commit ourselves to the purchase of a small fortune in tools, new suits, or membership in scientific organizations, and then get fired for poor work, we are learning the hard way that we didn't pass the test. Several such mishaps may convince us to volunteer for the U.S. Army, or maybe even the French Foreign Legion.

The best way to look at testing is as a means of saving ourselves time, money, and ego. Tests are not designed to embarrass, but to guide us toward a proper career. A young man of high IQ decided that his future lay in the field of dental surgery. He wanted to be paid well for his efforts and the pay was obviously good. His work would also be a needed service to his fellow man and, finally, he thought it would be pleasant to play golf on Thursdays as well as on weekends. Unfortunately, well along in his premed course he found not only that his hands were too large, but also that he could not stand the sight of blood! Being a low-handicap golfer with intelligence and a taste for the good life is no guarantee of success as a dental surgeon.

AN INTELLIGENT LOOK AT IQ

Some sort of intelligence measurement is generally part of the battery of tests used to determine a person's qualifi-

cations for an occupation. Do you know *your* IQ? Few of us do, and the reason generally given is that educators don't want to risk doing more harm than good. A young genius might lord it over less-gifted friends, and the less-gifted might be hurt to know that they were in that category. It has also been charged that IQ testing doesn't accurately measure intelligence. At the moment, intelligence tests are under a cloud, but many businesses have long used them and believe they work. Performance results over many years indicate that this is so.

IQ stands for "intelligence quotient." It is intended to be a measure of individual intelligence compared to average intelligence. Such tests have been given to hundreds of millions of people, and fixed standards have been established. A score of 100 indicates that a person is of average intelligence. A score above 140 ranks him a genius; 60 suggests that he is seriously deficient mentally.

A recent criticism of intelligence tests is that they handicap those who are lacking in language mastery or have had little experience with the examples used in the test questions. Obviously a foreigner, or a person isolated from social and cultural advantages, would have little idea what was being asked, and could not make correct responses. It is true that disadvantaged people do not score as well on the average. Some say that for this reason we cannot expect as much from these people, or even that we should reject the whole concept of intelligence testing as unfair and unrealistic. However, testing in real-life situations is going to continue, whatever we do about IQ tests. There are certain mental requirements for certain jobs, and those who don't have them cannot perform satisfactorily.

To screen candidates for various air-crew positions during World War II, the U.S. Army Air Corps used a very thorough series of tests: intelligence, manual dexterity, vision, hearing, aptitudes, interests, and so on. The predictive ability of these tests was remarkably accurate. Pilots, navigators, and bombardiers who scored high in testing generally did well in training and functioned satisfactorily as air-crew members; those who scored low were most prone to "wash out" of training. Since hundreds of thousands of cadets participated, the correlations between testing and actual performance were not based on coincidence.

Even larger samples have been obtained in the Army and Navy, and again there is good correlation between test scores and performance; this time in the reverse situation. People coming from different vocations in civilian life score differently in the Army General Classification Test. Over the years, teachers ranged from 110 to 140 while farmers scored from 61 to 115. Highest scores were made by accountants, who ranged from 115 to 143; the lowest by lumberjacks who scored from 60 to 115.

It might be argued that teachers would naturally score higher, since they are involved with a great variety of knowledge in their day-to-day work. However, it has been found that a person's intelligence remains remarkably constant from childhood to maturity. Furthermore, even specific coaching on intelligence tests produces only a temporary increase in scores, and only on the particular test used. Imperfect as IQ tests may be, they consistently measure something of an individual's mental abilities.

The criticism is made that intelligence testing tends to put people into certain categories, with little room for flexibility. However, note that in the example above some farmers scored 115 and so did some accountants. On the average, however, accountants scored 125 while farmers scored about 88. This is much different, of course, than saying that one *must* be a shipping clerk if he scores 110. It happens that 110 *was* the average score for shipping clerks, but scores ranged all the way from 87 to 127. Not every clerk-typist has a score of 105, and not all airplane pilots score 120. Some manual laborers rank higher than 100, and some people in higher-level jobs have lower scores. An intelligence test score is an indicator, a gauge of potential ability, but it is by no means the only factor. In general, testers believe that those with high IQ scores *will* succeed if they apply themselves. Those with low scores *may* succeed, but require more motivation than those with higher scores.

HOW'S YOUR APTITUDE?

Intelligence tests generally measure verbal comprehension, mathematical ability, and spatial thinking. They do not include special aptitudes like musical ability, manual dexterity (these two go together in making a successful musician), or mechanical, clerical, athletic, artistic, and social aptitudes. Separate aptitude or skill tests have proved useful over many years of experience. An example is the Seashore Test. Named for its developer, it was designed to measure musical ability. Do you believe that

anyone can be a musician if he wants to and applies himself diligently to the piano bench or guitar pick? Unfortunately, this is not the case, even if he is a genius, for aptitudes do not necessarily go along with intelligence.

Other physiological abilities can also be accurately tested. Hearing is one of these. Not only musicians but people in some other fields too need accurate hearing. Color vision is important, as well, and some states will not license drivers who are color blind. Color blindness is a hereditary variation in an individual. Try as he will, he cannot tell colors apart, just as some of us cannot tell one note from another.

A MATTER OF INTEREST

In addition to aptitude tests, there are interest tests. The Strong Vocational Interest Blank and the Thurstone Primary Interest Test are examples, as are the Minnesota and the Kuder tests. These psychological tests can even tell us things about ourselves that we are not consciously aware of, and probably could not find out otherwise.

A word of caution about taking interest tests: With intelligence tests or aptitude tests it is difficult to score too high, although it is possible to get an erroneously *low* score by being tired or emotionally upset, or by deliberately doing poorly. Not so with the interest test. Often there is a tendency to put down what we think are the "right" answers. What this really does, of course, is lessen the accuracy of the test. So answer as honestly as you can, whether it seems the right answer or not. Attempts to fool the tester may well lead to an "interest profile" that is of no help to anyone.

Don't let tests or test givers snow you, and don't let a test score wreck your ego or your career plans. Tests are *not* infallible; use them not as commands but as guidelines or maps of your potential. Knowing your IQ, you can check to see if it lies in the range established for the business, skill, or profession you seem interested in. If your counselor cautions against entering social work because your interest profile suggests you will not do well working with people, at least give some attention to his warning. Maybe the interest test is wrong; maybe you can get along as a case worker or counselor in spite of the indicated lack of empathy. But be aware that such a career will be more difficult than if you sincerely enjoyed helping people.

The counselor may provide you with an interest profile, and also suggestions for your vocation. For example, I was told that my interest profile indicated success in the fields of publishing and aviation. My vocation now is writing and my avocation is flying a sailplane. I was also cautioned against social work, or any kind of work involving personal dealings with people. I know that it was good advice, for I have learned through experience that I work best alone.

PUTTING TESTS TO WORK

Start with your own evaluation of yourself. By now you should be aware of your likes, dislikes, and skills, and you probably also have some idea of your mental ability. Your performance on tests and how you measure up with your friends in various tasks should indicate if you are about average, a little brighter, or not quite as sharp as most others. You should check these self-tests with more formal tests of various kinds. Here are some examples.

If your father and mother were both musicians, you have always wanted to be one, your interest tests bear this out, your Seashore and Kwalwasser-Dykma tests show that you have absolute pitch and score in the 100th percentile in all other categories, and your IQ is 150, you don't have much of a problem. But suppose you come from a family of nonmusicians and just think you would like to be a musician. Now your musical aptitude scores are more critical. You find that you did only so-so in these tests; not bad but not really red-hot either. Interest tests show that you really lean more to mechanical work. Your manual dexterity is great, which could be helpful either in music or in mechanical work. Your IQ is at about the center of the range for either musician or toolmaker. You had always considered metalworking only as a hobby; now you might better think of it as your career, with music as the hobby. There is also the knowledge that *as a rule* a toolmaker makes more money and is more steadily employed than a musician (and your interest profile showed that security is of importance to you). Of course you can still try to make it as a musician if you want, because your scores are into the success bracket, although just barely in some categories.

Let's take another case. You have always been interested in computers and feel that there is a great future in this field. You have even built a simple electronic compu-

ter, and although math is difficult, you have persevered and learned a good bit about programming. So you decide to take a battery of intelligence, interest, and aptitude tests.

The results are hard to believe and you feel they must be wrong: you scored very low in the math portions of the intelligence test; your aptitude and interest tests indicate that you would be a poor risk as a programmer, much less a computer analyst. IQ-wise you are at the low end of the range for analysts. Surprisingly, you scored very high in the personality department, with most of the attributes of the successful salesman or advertising manager! So maybe you should begin to reorient your thinking and planning toward a career of *selling* computers, or selling something else that interests you.

The matter of using tests or not using them is probably going to be pretty much up to you. Far from being forced to take tests of your intelligence, interests, and aptitudes, you may not have them offered to you. As an example, because of pressures from those opposed to invasion of personal privacy many tests can no longer be given to U.S. Civil Service candidates and employees. Furthermore, if you do manage to take such tests, no one will try to force you to make use of the results. To test or not to test; it's your choice. Just remember that testing in one form or another takes place somewhere along the line. If not early, it will come later—maybe too late to do you much good.

LET IGNORANCE TALK AS IT WILL,
LEARNING HAS ITS VALUE.

Jean de la Fontaine
Book VIII; Fable 19,
The Use of Knowledge

What School Can Do For You

Education is a $100-billion-a-year business involving 52 million students and 10 million educators. It is here to stay, and probably will increase in scope and cost as well as in the effect it has on our lives. The purposes of education can be defined in many ways, and different people have different ideas about what it should do. Here are several basic goals generally suggested:

The teaching of reading, writing, and arithmetic
An introduction to cultural values, including art, literature, and music
An opportunity for each student to learn to best use his talents and abilities
Preparation for a useful and rewarding occupation

The development of qualities that will make students useful citizens.

There was a time when no one went to school or even knew what a school was. Life itself was school enough; young people learned from their elders, from the environment, and from accident and experiment. "Learning by doing," was about the only kind of education available before the coming of indoctrination, initiation, and other special rites relating to the gods and demons primitive peoples worshipped.

EDUCATION = CIVILIZATION

Formal learning was originally only for men and boys. In primitive societies girls were instructed in domestic duties by their mothers, older sisters, and other women of the tribe. Boys were trained to hunt, to fight, and also to participate in magic and religious rites. The first schools, then, were for males, and this formal education was often available only to the upper-class males, the rulers of a society. The sons of this class were destined by divine right (or more realistically by political or military muscle) to be educated so that they in their turn could rule the country and lead it in war.

The involvement of religion in education has continued until present times. Perhaps you attend a parochial school, or have friends who do. Many of the great universities were founded by religious organizations, and some continue their church affiliation. However, early in the history of our country it was decided that state governments, rather than the church, should operate the schools. The federal government over the last few decades has also become increasingly involved in education. This is an indication of how important our government considers education. Indeed, the strength and productivity of a society depends in very large part on the education of its members. Although we are blessed with a wealth of natural resources in America, it has taken more than raw materials to make the kind of society we live in today. Educated people created the United States, and we need to keep our population educated in order to keep the country going and to make continuing progress. Our goal, then, is to educate not just men and boys, not just the wealthy, powerful, or most intelligent, but to educate *all* the people.

THE THREE R'S

In spite of objections to spending twelve or more years in classrooms when we would much rather be outside enjoying life, most of us agree that it is useful to read and write fairly well and to be able to do arithmetic. Some few people sign their name with an X, cannot read, and have not progressed beyond two plus two is four. But as a practical matter, we need the three R's in our daily life.

An early ruler of Egypt, presented by his priests with a system of written communication, refused to let it be made available to his subjects. His reason: They would no longer have to think for themselves but would rely on something already written down. The ruler preferred to stick to

"real" things, rather than teach his people to read and
write symbols. Such a view could not hold out long
against the power of written communication, of course,
and literacy has long been a measure of human progress.
Unfortunately, not all of us measure up.

It is a tragedy that some students reach college unable to
read properly. Sometimes there are physiological reasons
for this shortcoming. Failures in reading can sometimes be
blamed on poor teaching, or on a lack of emphasis on
reading. But much of the blame must fall on the individual
who simply does not make enough effort to learn to read.
Reading, like most other skills, is a two-way street;
teacher and student both must work at the learning process
if it is to be successful. The best teacher in the world cannot force a person to learn very much. A problem also
exists when we have a willing student but a poor teacher.
Here the situation is easier, however, for it is generally

possible to find a good teacher somewhere. It is also possible to learn much on one's own. Books and other materials can be teachers; television can be a teaching tool; and tape recorders are being used increasingly in education. None of these completely take the place of "old Socrates," the master teacher, but they help.

An eager student *and* an eager teacher can work wonders; if the world were filled with both it would be a better educated and happier world. However, it won't help much to reach a crucial point in your life and complain to anyone who will listen that you had a rotten teacher who didn't motivate you. That may be true, but you should have motivated yourself. In those cases where it *was* the educator's fault, the result is the same: The illiterate student is poorly prepared, or not prepared at all, for the world he enters from school.

It is no coincidence that reading is first of the three R's. We think in words, and until we can learn words it is difficult to learn anything else. Some things can be taught verbally but many cannot; all can be better taught if the printed word is used in the teaching process. So the nonreader or the poor reader must achieve at least minimum reading ability to succeed in a literate society.

Writing is to reading as speaking is to listening, and "Speak for yourself" is good advice. You may hire a résumé-writing firm to help you get a job, but the day may come when you yourself must write to keep the job. Today a farmer has to be able to write and so does a plumber. You may never write the Great American Novel (although a great many people dream about doing that) but you are at least going to have to write letters from time to time and maybe reports or suggestions at work.

The computer has not taken over, in spite of rumors to the contrary, and even nonmathematicians are called on to do a certain amount of arithmetic. We live in a check-writing world, and although we make jokes about not being able to balance the checkbook it is not really a joke. Neither is it a joke when a young couple suddenly realize they are committed to monthly payments totaling a hundred dollars more than they earn.

The person who has paid attention in math class and learned to add, subtract, multiply, and divide is far happier at tax time, budget time, shopping time, investment time, and many other times. In the kitchen, a working knowledge of mathematics can make recipes handy directions instead of hopelessly confusing formulas.

MAKING THE BEST OF EACH DAY

Even if you do not accept the fact that you need reading, writing, and arithmetic—even if you argue that computers can do all the math you need, and that if you can speak and understand English you can get by—you are still stuck with formal education. For all state laws insist that you attend school until a certain age, usually until you are fourteen or sixteen. Like it or not; you will spend from eight to twenty years inside the ivy halls, or walls, of learning.

Factory workers have been quoted as complaining, "We have to *be* here for eight hours every day—you don't really expect us to work too?'' Unfortunately some students adopt the same approach to school. Refusing to apply themselves, they often spend more effort than would be required for proper study. Sometimes such rebels become millionaires and confound the teachers who predicted a bleak future for them. But such success stories are unusual, and the illiterate generally must settle for such menial tasks as digging ditches. Most of us want to do better than that.

Europeans have a system that eliminates much of the decision-making from education. The brainy, or the rich, take an educational track toward a life of prestige, power, or ease. The less brainy, or the poor, are educated on another educational track for nonprofessional employment. This is a very practical system, in that it works. It is also a class system bound to make mistakes and hurt many people. India, in its caste system, has carried such a social approach farther than other countries. While people of the lower castes in India sometimes do rise to high position, it is much more difficult to make the transition there than in a freer society.

Our system makes mistakes too, perhaps as many as the rigid systems that preselect early in life and then mold young people for a particular job. Surely our system is very expensive. More importantly, it places a greater burden on the individual student: Your future depends largely on the decisions *you* make and the effort *you* devote to carrying out those decisions. Taxpayers pay the money but you make the choice. You can rock along on ''social promotion,'' or drop out, and you won't go to jail or even be

thought of too harshly. However, there may come a day
when you wish you had learned more while ''serving your
time'' in elementary and high school classes.

Going to school is something like breathing; you have to
do it. So if you've got to be there, you might as well make
good use of your time. Look around. Talk with your
teachers, and even with administrators—who may be more
interested than you think. Participate in extracurricular activities on campus, of which there are usually many.
Drama club, school newspaper, magazine or yearbook
staff, Spanish club, science club, tennis or debate team,
and so on. If nothing in particular grabs you, flip a coin or
shut your eyes and pick something at random. At worst
you will waste a little time, although even finding out you
dislike debating is *not* a waste of time but a clue that you
probably would not make a good lawyer.

There was no music class or band for students in any of
the grade schools I attended. Today things are different.
My eleven-year-old daughter plays trombone and doubles
on key bass in the band, has another music class, and is
still so interested in music that she takes piano outside
school and plays the recorder for fun. Should she decide to
make music a career, she has the jump on someone who
decides belatedly that music is his cup of tea. At the least,
she is developing an appreciation for music, something
that no amount of money can buy. Are you learning to
play an instrument, or singing in a glee club, choir, or
quartet?

A CAREER IN SPORTS

Physical education is education too. Long ago, and again wisely, those in charge of education decided that physical fitness was important. A Latin motto that may still be found carved on old gymnasiums is *"Mens sana in corpore sano"*: A healthy mind in a healthy body. While there are some mentally alert individuals who have difficulty touching their toes or lifting anything heavier than a cocktail glass, and some athletes are low in IQ, these are generally the exception and not the rule. Physical health is much desired, and the School Physical Fitness program inaugurated by President Kennedy typifies the belief that education should do more for students than teach them the three R's and a few social graces. It is possible that your career may lie in some sport. While it is difficult to believe that anything as pleasant as playing golf, tennis, or football is work, many students later find these rewarding careers. Give sports a hard look. Making it as a golf pro or a basketball coach may be tougher than succeeding as an engineer but if you are cut out for sports you may never be happy as an engineer.

While in school you have a great opportunity to get the experience necessary for entry into professional sports. Pro baseball, football, and basketball each year sign up appreciable numbers of young athletes who have proved themselves in high school or college. Colleges recruit from high schools and offer scholarships that give an athlete four years of further training—plus formal education to go with it. At the end of that time scouts are eagerly watching for pro material, ready with a contract if you can make the grade. Consider this career field carefully, if you haven't already.

THE TEACHING PROFESSION

As a student you also have a closeup seat to observe the teaching profession, a large and important part of the work world. Do you admire and respect your teachers and think you might enjoy teaching young people—or older people—as your career? There was a time when teaching was mainly a labor of love, for the pay was not all that great. Today teachers are better paid. You will be making a bad decision, however, if you tell yourself something like "I sure won't have a ball but it's a secure job with pretty good pay and steady increases." If your interest lies elsewhere, say in astronomy, medicine, or carpentry, better think twice. Of course you might take the best of both worlds and teach in your field of interest. Remember that teaching means you are committed to four years of higher education, and probably some years beyond that for an advanced degree.

VOCATIONAL EDUCATION

Do names like DECA, FBLA, FFA, FHA, OEA, and VICA ring any bells with you? If you are serious about a career they should. For each of these school organizations helps prepare students for interesting occupations.

DECA stands for Distributive Education Clubs of America, and serves students in marketing, merchandising, and management courses. Often DECA students work half the school day on a real job in their field of interest.

FBLA stands for Future Business Leaders of America. Affiliated with Phi Beta Lambda, this national organization serves students interested in careers in the business world.

FFA is the Future Farmers of America, for students seeking careers in agriculture, mechanics, natural resources, environmental science, horticulture, and forestry.

FHA stands for Future Homemakers of America. It serves those enrolled in home economics and related courses.

OEA is the Office Education Association, for students taking courses in office work.

VICA stands for Vocational Industrial Clubs of America, and serves students taking trade, industrial, technical, and health education courses.

There are other vocational organizations, including 4H and Junior Achievement. If you are not familiar with what these programs offer, find out from your counselor. No need to miss a good bet while there is still time to get involved. We will talk about vocational education more in Chapter 7.

COUNSELING

Counseling is a part of education, and you should get as much guidance as you can. Sometimes this may be difficult, for counselors generally have more students assigned to them than they can properly help. This is especially true when much counseling has to be devoted to behavior problems.

I have been on the receiving end of much guidance that was not particularly helpful. In junior college the band director was my counselor. As he was first to point out, he was not particularly well qualified to advise English majors. I have also heard many horror stories about career guidance—and believe most of them. The following is a quote from President Johnson's 1965 "Manpower Report" :

Of every ten high school dropouts, eight reported that they had never been counselled by a school official or by a public employment office about job training or the kind of work to look for. Even among high school graduates, less than half reported that they had received occupational guidance.

At the very least, your school should be able to provide an opportunity for you to take intelligence, aptitude, and interest tests. If you already have taken some of these, your counselor can make results available during your meetings with him. Some schools have aggressive testing and counseling programs, on a compulsory basis. Many do not, and such help is available only if you seek it out, often at some effort on your part. It is worth the trouble, however, for your career may be at stake.

EDUCATION AND EARNINGS

As an indication of the importance of education, here are figures comparing amount of education with expected lifetime income, estimated for a recent year.

Four years or more of college	$366,900
One to three years of college	269,105
High school graduation	215,487
One to three years of high school	175,779
Elementary school graduation	149,687
Less than eight years of school	106,449

In the same year, the *average* unemployment rate was 4.4 percent. However, the rate varied considerably with the

amount of education a person had, as the following figures
show.

	percentage
Sixteen or more years of school	1.4
Thirteen to fifteen years	3.1
Twelve	3.4
Nine to eleven	6.7
Eight	5.2
Five to seven	6.5
Less than five years	7.1
Average	4.4

It has been pointed out that statistics can be made to
support anything—including the men who put together the
statistics. We will consider education and earnings again in
Chapter 8; however, common sense suggests that if all
other things are equal, the person with better education
will be better prepared to succeed in his job. School can be
a bummer, or it can help make your life rewarding. You
are a large factor in what it will be.

WHY SHOULDN'T WE DEVELOP THE ATTITUDE THAT IT IS ALSO
RESPECTABLE TO BE A PLUMBER OR AN ELECTRICIAN, OR, FOR
THAT MATTER, A CUSTODIAN? THESE JOBS NEED TO BE DONE, AND
DONE WELL, BY PEOPLE WHO HAVE PRIDE IN THEIR WORK AND
WHO ARE RESPECTED BY THEIR FELLOW CITIZENS. COULD CAREER
EDUCATION HELP US CHANGE OUR ATTITUDES? I THINK THE ANSWER
IS YES.

Larry Allen
1972 high school graduate
and past president Vocational
Industrial Clubs of America

Career
Education

In general there are three "tracks" a student may take in
his high school career. One track is vocational education.
For a variety of reasons, only a handful of students take
courses of this kind. Another track is known vaguely as
"general education," designed to impart basic skills. Another handful take such programs. By far the most popular
is the "academic" track, intended to prepare the student
for further education at the college or university level.

VOCATIONAL EDUCATION

We have noted that the Egyptians were aware of vocational guidance 4,500 years ago, and that Plato was among the ancient Greek scholars who stressed the importance of helping talent to flourish. The Hebrew scholar Maimonides in the twelfth century wrote that it was society's responsibility to teach each person a trade or business so that he might "earn an honest livelihood, and not be forced to the dreadful alternative of holding out his hand for charity."

Vocational education was practiced by pioneer Americans long before they organized schools to teach their children. Early schoolmasters and schoolmistresses were expected to teach their students reading, writing, and arithmetic. Not how to plow a straight furrow, plant seed the proper depth, burn stumps, or move rocks. The vocational part of education was still taught at home.

As our country changed from an agricultural economy to one involving business and industry, however, jobs came into being for which parents could not train their children. Automobile mechanics, steam engineering, telegraphy, and stenography are examples of work which earlier generations had no knowledge of. The importance of this change in the work world was evident even on the political scene. Here is part of the platform of the Workingmen's Party in 1830:

Instead of the mind being exclusively cultivated at the expense of the body or the body slavishly

overwrought to the injury of the mind, they [the Workingmen's Party] hope to see a nation of equal fellow citizens, all trained to produce and all permitted to enjoy. As the first and chief of their objectives, therefore, the mechanics and workingmen put forward a system of Equal, Republican, Scientific, Practical Education.

Vocational training began in American schools before 1900, aimed at teaching students to be craftsmen, tradesmen, office workers, and so on. With the shift away from traditional European inheritance laws, the coming of estate taxes, and the growth of a variety of new job opportunities, fewer young people followed in the footsteps of their parents. A boy from a long line of farmers might decide to build automobiles or steamboats. A girl whose mother and grandmother had been schoolteachers might want to go to the city and work in an office. Books were published on vocational education and choosing a career. There was also much interest at the federal level, and Congress in 1917 passed the Smith-Hughes Act, setting up cooperation between federal government and the states for promotion and development of vocational education.

However, even though our country saw the need for vocational training more than a century ago, such programs still benefit only a small percentage of students. Part of the reason is the philosophy of giving everyone a chance to reach the top. This is a noble goal, although we might question the definition of "the top." But what happens to those who miss the top and must settle for something less than bank president or senior computer designer?

Somewhere along the way, vocational education came to be considered a last resort for students who couldn't make it in a college preparatory program. The slow learners, the poverty-stricken, and the minorities were the students shunted into "voc ed," or trade school. Somehow vocational education even became linked by association with reform schools where youthful delinquents were rehabilitated by being taught a trade.

As a result, all that many parents would accept in the way of vocational education were courses in woodworking or "manual training," where the student built a better birdhouse, or a beautifully sandpapered and varnished plywood winding reel for kite string. There was auto shop, of course, but many students took that class only so that they could work on their own hot rods and save money. Auto mechanics, in the eyes of many, were grubby types with greasy hands, who lived across the tracks.

Instead of being a part of the overall school program, vocational education sometimes was taught at separate "trade schools." These were often in a poor part of town, close to the students who could not hope to profit from the "liberal" education given to those who were better off. Too often the philosophy seemed to be to let the blacks, the Mexicans, the poor, and the retarded take voc ed so they could do the dirty work for society.

Unfortunately, many educators adopted the view that a student who decided he wanted to take this "low road" indicated a failure on the part of teachers and counselors (who had tried so hard to inspire the student to go on to State U or Eastern Tech). Any worthwhile young American was expected to embark on an academic program to prepare for the college of one's own choice (or perhaps the choice of one's parents)—this in spite of a world of work that offered professional positions to only about one employee in seven. Education became a game of musical chairs in which not one, but *most,* participants failed to find a seat. And often they landed on the hard floor with a painful thump.

TROUBLE IN PARADISE

We could spend a lot of time arguing about the right approach for education, and even about its proper goals. Perhaps the simplest way of deciding is to look around us and see if we are satisfied with the results. After many decades of a system which sought to give everyone a chance to pursue a higher education, our nation is the richest, most powerful, and influential in the world. However, it is also true that about 11 percent of those leaving our schools between eighteen and twenty-five years of age are out of work; that 850,000 of them drop out of school every year; and that another 1,650,000 leave school each year without job preparation of some sort.

There are 18 million illiterates in our country. Since this is about one in ten of those old enough to read and write, the problem is obviously a very serious one. Although there are jobs that such people can do, it is a disservice to society at large, and the affected individuals in particular, for the educational system to have failed so drastically with such a large proportion of our students.

There may be a lesson for us in the fact that the average student at the Los Angeles Trade Technical College (who is in his twenties) has gone through ten jobs before enrolling at the college. Another indication of a problem is the number of training programs that business and industry operate at their own expense to train new employees, or prospective employees. Too often, many businessmen point out, applicants come seeking jobs without the knowledge and skills they will need in such work. It seems unbelievable that banks should have to train their help in arithmetic, grammar, and spelling, but they do. In spite of the high cost in dollars, facilities, personnel, and time, there seems no other way to get enough properly trained employees. Indeed, it has been suggested that this may be the method of education in the future, with each business or industry operating its own job-training programs for new help. Naturally the pay for trainees is less than the regular pay, and sometimes there is no more compensation than the instruction itself. If businesses *could* get qualified help, they could save money, and the new worker could earn a better salary for his efforts.

CAREER EDUCATION

Whether work is richly rewarding or demeaning, the fact remains that most of us are going to work for a living. Which brings us to the concept of "career education"— conscious, formal preparation for the world we must live in. Dr. James Conant, who had carefully studied education in America, wrote this in 1961:

I submit that in a heavily urbanized and industrialized free society the educational experiences of youth should fit their subsequent employment. There should be a smooth transition from full-time schooling to a full-time job, whether that transition be after grade 10 or after graduation from high school, college, or university.

Many concerned Americans agreed with Dr. Conant about this educational responsibility. Among them was Governor James Rhodes of Ohio, who decided that something should be done for the six of every seven Ohio students who would find no room at the "higher levels" of employment: His state accelerated its vocational education program to prepare students for a job upon graduation. Here was effort at the individual state level, but the problem was also being approached from the top of government.

In March of 1970 President Nixon asked educators to design educational reforms for the decade of the seventies. One response to this challenge was the proposal of Dr. Sidney Marland, who was then commissioner of education. According to Dr. Marland, students in schools throughout the United States complained that their courses were dull and irrelevant and that their education did not open the way to a fulfilling adult life. Low achievement scores, high dropout rates, vandalism, drug abuse, and violence also pointed strongly to student discontent.

In 1970 only one student in six was taking public school courses that would prepare him for the real world of work. Questioning the idea that our nation could afford to encourage practically all to pursue academic courses while neglecting those who would fill the majority of our jobs, Dr. Marland suggested:

> Educators must be bent on preparing students either to become properly and usefully employed immediately upon graduation from high school or to go on to fur-

ther formal education. The student should be equipped occupationally, academically, and emotionally to spin off from the system at whatever point he chooses—whether at age sixteen as a craftsman apprentice, or age thirty as a surgeon, or age sixty as a newly trained practical nurse.

The "career education" idea took hold quickly, and a number of states already have active programs aimed at graduating students prepared to enter the work world immediately if they so desire. According to its proponents, career education is not an attempt to determine in advance exactly how many job openings there are and how many employees are needed in each and then to force young people into those the government feels they best fit. Instead, career education seeks to make students aware of the world

of work and of their own interests and abilities and to help them "learn a living."

Long before the current career education movement, there were educational programs to prepare students for careers, of course. For all its shortcomings, vocational education has trained many young people for a job upon graduation. But it reaches only a small percentage of the school population. Career education is not just a new name for vocational education. It includes traditional vocational courses but also offers other courses to those not interested in such occupations. Students are also taught how our economic system works, the part they play in it, and the variety of jobs that are available.

To get the new career education concept started, federal funds were offered to schools with programs designed to prepare students for an occupation. Arizona was first to pass a law implementing career education, and a variety of programs began to blossom all over the country.

Career education exploded suddenly on the school scene and it was some time before educators were ready to question the concept. But when they came, the questions were serious: Wouldn't this reduce college enrollment? Would it not be the "death of intellect in the West?" Wasn't this really the pigeonholing of students early in life for certain jobs, decided upon by Department of Labor predictions of industry and other needs?

Dr. Marland's answer to charges that he would de-intellectualize the nation is that knowledge for its own sake is meaningless. By making knowledge relevant to the real world of work, career education will spark an even greater interest in knowledge:

It is important that each student master the skills he will require to live by. Whether these skills are labeled "academic" or "vocational" is beside the point. The essential need is that every student be equipped to live his life as a fulfilled human being. If he is to live his life with machines, he must know how to use them. If he is to live with a slide rule or a computer, he must understand its magic. If he is to combat diseases that afflict mankind, he must know a great deal about the human body and mind and all the ills they are heir to.

THE CHOICE IS YOURS

Except for a small fraction of the total student population, our school system has largely left career education for the student himself to accomplish—sometimes *after* he has completed twelve or even sixteen years of schooling. This approach, whatever its merits, has often resulted in frustration and delay at the very least, and failure and despair at worst. With an oversupply of "higher-level" graduates (many of them not properly trained in their intended field), the country is short of trained office and industry personnel, technical workers, and other nonprofessionals. Belatedly we are learning that college or university education is not always a guarantee of any job, much less a prestige position.

Career education is still a concept without a specific blueprint. But progress has been made and many schools are at least thinking about it. The chances for getting useful career education in school are surely better now than a decade ago. Even vocational education is not under the cloud it once was, and the notion that there is nothing bad about learning how to do a job is spreading.

THE EDUCATIONAL MYTH IS A SPIN-OFF OF THE SCHOOL MYTH. IT HOLDS THAT IF YOU HAVE ENOUGH DEGREES YOU WILL MAKE ENOUGH MONEY. THIS MYTH ORIGINATED IN THE "GOLDEN AGE" OF EDUCATION FOLLOWING WORLD WAR II. THERE WAS A GREAT DEMAND FOR TEACHERS TO TEACH THE NUMEROUS YOUNG, TO PRE-PARE HEADS FOR THE EGG-HEADED ECONOMY, AND TO OUTSPUTNIK THE SPUTNIK. THERE WAS A FREE FLOW OF MONEY TO EDUCATION FROM GOVERNMENT, FROM FOUNDATIONS, AND FROM PARENTS WHO DID NOT WANT THEIR KIDS TO BE LEFT OUT. THERE WAS A RAPID EXPANSION OF THE VISUAL-AURAL TRADES: ADVERTISING, PSYCHOANALYSIS, THEATER, STEREO, SOCIAL WORK, AND COMMU-NICATION. AS B.A.S MULTIPLIED TO QUALIFY PEOPLE FOR THE HEADY SOCIETY, IT BECAME NECESSARY TO GET THE M.A., AND THE PH.D. THEORETICALLY, THERE WAS NO END TO THIS BECAUSE KNOWLEDGE IS A COMMODITY THAT CAN BE CONSUMED—UNLIKE FUDGE SUNDAES—WITHOUT END. ACTUALLY, HOWEVER, THE LIMIT CAME MUCH SOONER THAN EXPECTED, AND BY 1970 COLLEGE-BRED LABOR GLUTTED THE MARKET. MEANWHILE A REAL SHORTAGE OF STONE MASONS EXISTED.

Gus Tyler
assistant president
International Garment Workers Union

The College Choice

College may be vital to your career, the only educational route to your chosen field. If you want to be a teacher, you must earn your degree in education. Should you decide to be a scientist, you must have college or university training. The same requirement applies to engineering, medicine, and other professions. Even in business it usually pays to earn a degree in business management, accounting, or economics.

Of course, many people receive college degrees, or at least some schooling at that level, yet take jobs that do not require college preparation. Certainly there are more benefits to be gained in college than credentials for a job. Association with others, including those of the opposite sex, makes higher learning more rewarding. Sports provide the motivation for some whose primary aim in college is not a degree. Exposure to cultural aspects of life is another important plus in education. Art, music, and literature are examples. So are foreign language studies and visits to other parts of the world, and college courses sometimes include such travel. These cultural experiences can help produce individuals who contribute more to society.

There was a time, as we have noted, when only the brilliant or wealthy attended college or university. Later, in Europe, there were two kinds of students. Some were in college to become lawyers, doctors, ministers, or other professionals. But there was another group, of wealthy young men, who were in college for an entirely different reason. Often they did not even seek grades for their efforts; higher learning for them was a combination finishing school and lawn party. Much of their education was obtained by travel abroad, with the added excitement of vacation and romance. There are some students like this in our country, using college for four years of good times,

excitement, and partying. But for most of us, life is more serious. While college can be pleasant, it serves higher purposes, among them the preparation for a meaningful career.

GO-TO-COLLEGE LOCKSTEP

Not long ago college was the "in" thing. Since failure to go was almost an admission that one was a second-class citizen, much money and effort were expended toward seeing that everyone went to college. The push came from many different sources. Educators hailed higher learning as one of our individual rights, as well as a benefit to society as a whole. Next were the students themselves, eager to qualify for rewarding occupations and also to enjoy the good life away from home. Parents also exerted much pressure, even on young people who were not red-hot on the idea of four more years of books. Another reason for college attendance was the threat of the draft.

A fifth source of pressure was business, which began to ask for higher education on jobs that earlier had required only high school diplomas. On the face of it, this seemed a logical requirement. Surely a person with four years of further study would be better prepared for a career in business, and businessmen had long been concerned about the lack of qualifications of some new employees. Unfortunately, this basically good idea has miscarried, with unwanted results that no one could foresee.

It is difficult to know how many jobs calling for college training really require that sort of education. For example, the Carnegie Commission on Higher Education in a 1973 report mentioned the "necessity for the absorption of some college-educated persons into jobs which have not been traditionally filled by persons with a college education." Postal positions were given as an example of this sort of "credentialism," the artificial setting of standards beyond those needed for a job or position. The obvious bad feature of such a practice is the waste of time and money earning these credentials. But a worse drawback was discovered.

It is to be expected that college-trained persons may take a first job below their educational level in order to gain practical knowledge. However, it has been found that many such trainees *remain* underemployed. They are far more capable than their jobs demand, yet not well-enough paid for their ability. As a result, they become dissatisfied and tend to move to another job as soon as they can. Thus credentialism is harmful to business as well as to frustrated employees.

THE HIGH COST OF HIGHER EDUCATION

It is possible to overdo any good thing. If four years of college can make a major contribution to a student, and to society as a whole, then it does seem that all of us should remain students through the first third of our lives. But there are problems, disadvantages, and costs (in time and money) that should be carefully considered. For some, four additional years of academic studies are delightful, productive, and well worth acquiring. For others, much of the time is a crashing bore, with college becoming as much a prison as elementary and high school sometimes seem to young people cooped up year after year. Probably the greatest cost is damage to the human spirit. But the financial cost must be weighed too.

Four years of college tuition is expensive. So are living expenses for that length of time. Add to these sums the amount of money that you could have earned in those four or more years, and you get some idea of the high cost of

higher learning. A conservative total of $50,000 suggests the cost in dollars alone. For many people, their early twenties should be years of productivity and accomplishment, not merely a continuation of the twelve years of school they have already completed.

In Chapter 6 it was suggested that a college education can mean an additional $150,000 earned during your working life. Since this is about $3,500 of extra income per·working year, it would seem that anyone who doesn't go to college just can't be very smart! However, we should not accept such promises at face value without some serious thinking about them. For example, it is generally the brighter students who complete college, and there is a demonstrated correlation between brightness and income. Many college graduates who earn a good income would have done so even without college.

One of the few millionaires I have known personally did not complete high school. Isolated cases like this prove nothing statistically, of course. But it is also true that in 1970 there were 2.7 million college graduates who earned less than $8,000, while 1.9 million high school graduates earned more than that amount. This does not mean that all high school graduates did better than all college graduates, of course. On the average, college graduates earn about 50 percent more than high school graduates. This is largely true because doctors, lawyers, and other very highly paid professionals must have college or university training. But we cannot all work in these fields, college degree or not. In the six of seven jobs *not* requiring higher education, a college diploma does not guarantee additional income, particularly when we subtract the thousands of dollars in educational costs and the four years without pay while in school.

A HARD SECOND LOOK

For many reasons, the college-for-everyone idea has been seriously challenged from a number of places. Perhaps the severest critics are students themselves who are wondering if they have been sold a bill of goods. Often the credentials they paid for with blood, sweat, and tears, plus many thousands of dollars and four or more of the best years of their lives are hardly worth the paper they are written on.

The Vietnam war is over, and the draft has been replaced by an all-volunteer military. There has always been criticism that it was unfair to spare those in college, while expecting sacrifices of those unable to attend. That hard choice no longer faces us, and there is less pressure on young people to take this route to avoid military service. Some writers believe that violence on American campuses in the 1960s came about at least in part because young people with energy and imagination were simply "imprisoned" in colleges and universities long past the time when they should have been *doing* something productive and rewarding. Whatever the reasons, a great change has occurred in evaluating college as to purposes and rewards.

Surveys taken in the spring of 1973 found that traditional pride in a college degree was waning, particularly among upper and middle classes. Many young people were putting off higher education until they "found themselves." In the twenty years from 1952 to 1972, college enrollments tripled under the go-to-college pressure. But by 1973 the enrollment increase was down to about 2 percent. In mid-April, the National Association of College Admissions Counselors estimated that there were more than 600,000 openings in colleges and universities, a sharp contrast to the very crowded conditions of prior years. Many colleges and universities have adopted the practice of going to high school campuses to "recruit" students.

Dramatic indications that something was wrong came

when a great oversupply of scientists and engineers resulted from government cutbacks in military, space, and other research areas. One young chemist in four in our country was unemployed. Of 200,000 new teachers graduated in June, 1972, more than 111,000 were still looking for positions the following year. And 10,000 lawyers who graduated in 1972 could not find work in the legal field. It is one thing to promise prestige positions for all; it is far more difficult to change the world enough to make that promise good.

Graduates with Ph.D. degrees are a glut on the market, with four or more applicants for each available position. As a result, mathematicians are reported managing hamburger shops, and geologists are doing stenographic work in newspaper offices. Senator Walter F. Mondale of Minnesota told the sad story of an honors graduate in biology from his state who could find no work and had to go on welfare. Meanwhile, many plumbers, masons, and other workers command wages that exceed the salaries of some professionals.

COLLEGE: IF YOU NEED IT

The decision by everyone to become a college graduate does not automatically and immediately create sufficient jobs to match these talents. If all of us attended college the world might be a better place. However, if we are considering college as the Open Sesame to highly paid, prestigious, and rewarding careers, then many of us are doomed to disappointment. The day may finally come when the only work available is for Ph.D.s, if computers and robots are doing everything else. But none of us are likely to be around when that automated society arrives. Indeed, predictions by experts are that in the year 2,000, when readers of this book will be enjoying their most productive years, the ratio of professional jobs to nonprofessional will remain about the same as it is today. And there will still be a need for some manual labor.

All colleges are not four-year institutions, of course. The junior college, or community college as it is now more popularly called, often is a successful compromise between no college and four or more years of it. Many two-year "terminal" courses prepare a student for direct entry into a job. Among such courses are medical technology, police science, many of the trades, sales, advertising, painting, and so on. Federal agencies suggest technical training for work available in civil engineering, health services, data processing, environmental control, forestry, and other areas. Requiring but one or two years of technical schooling which is often available at low cost in a nearby community college, such jobs pay as well as many "high-level" positions. Sometimes the pay is even better.

Higher learning is vital to modern society, and the nation that slights it is guilty of a blunder that will cost much in terms of human happiness and well-being. For some, college is an absolute necessity; for most it is an option to be decided on. It should be possible for each of us to make our own choice, based on our own needs, tastes, and abilities. *Make sure you go to college for the right reasons.*

OCCUPATIONAL CHOICE MAY DETERMINE WHETHER ONE IS EM-
PLOYED OR NOT; IT MAY DETERMINE HIS SUCCESS OR FAILURE; IT IN-
FLUENCES EVERY OTHER ASPECT OF LIFE, INCLUDING WHERE HOME
WILL BE, SCHOOLS AVAILABLE FOR CHILDREN, WHOM YOU WILL
WORK WITH, AND WHAT SORT OF SURROUNDINGS AND FRIENDS YOU
WILL HAVE. OCCUPATIONAL CHOICE ALSO DETERMINES HOW SOCIETY
AS A WHOLE WILL USE ITS PEOPLE.

Bruce E. Shertzer
Career Exploration and Planning

The Big Leap:
Getting a Job

Occasionally someone slides effortlessly into an important
job in the family corporation, a position he has been
groomed for since the day he was born. For most of us the
transition from student to employee is more difficult. And
getting a job, taking a position, going to work—whatever
we call the process—is one of the key decision points in
our lives. It makes sense, then, to assure ourselves of income, stature, happiness, and other desirables work can
provide.

Next to a tailor-made career through family or other
connections, perhaps the easiest route is through part-time

work that gradually becomes a full-time occupation. The DECA, VICA, and other similar programs mentioned earlier are typical of this gradual entry approach. You begin by helping with the bookkeeping in a local stationery store on weekends and afternoons. After two or three years of such part-time work, you feel that you would like to make this your vocation on a full-time basis. So you simply show up at work instead of school on Monday morning. Or you have helped out at a garage or filling station to earn spending money for several years and decide to work there full-time when high school years end.

Such a transition is fairly painless, with nothing new or frightening about the work. Since you have been doing the work successfully for some time there should be little chance of failure when it becomes a steady job. You are also familiar with the other employees and the boss. The main difference is that now you will work an eight-hour day and your check will be much larger than that received for a few hours part-time.

If you are still some distance from graduation and full-time employment, you might consider this "paving-the-way" method, particularly if you are sure what you want to do when you go to work. This approach doesn't always work, of course. It is possible that after several years of exposure to what you thought would be a great occupation, you get turned off. Or it may be that your future lies in a completely different occupation, and you have been doing this work for spending money only, with no intent of ever going into it as a career.

Some educational tracks are clear guidelines to specific

jobs. Engineering is an example. Such a career requires that you go on to college or university and complete four years or more of specialized study. In scientific and technical fields there are helpful guidelines along the way. Often your teachers can steer you to jobs. Sometimes industry, business, or government send recruiters to your school to see if you fit their needs, and to show what they have to offer you.

We know that the athlete who has been setting records during high school or college generally finds his path considerably smoothed. He may be literally taken by the hand from school to sports career, with a good contract to attest to his hard work and ability. A similar happy fate often befalls students in academic courses who demonstrate outstanding abilities. The young engineer whose designs have won competition after competition and the young botanist who has published a paper on the new plant she identified may find the red carpet laid out—perhaps in several different directions so that the toughest part is deciding which offer to accept! Not all of us are in "guaranteed treatment" categories, however, and more of the work of selling our abilities is going to fall on us. Instead of jobs coming to us, we generally must go ourselves to the people doing the hiring. It is an important part of the campaign.

The effectiveness of various methods of obtaining jobs is shown in these recently compiled statistics.

Direct application to employers	35%
Leads from relatives, friends, and other employees of firms	23%

State employment agencies   16%
"Help Wanted" advertisements   11%
Fee-charging employment agencies   4%
All other channels   11%

If you have not considered all these approaches, give them some thought. It is interesting to note that for every person hired through a professional agency, nine get jobs by contacting an employer on their own.

APPLYING FOR A JOB

There is an old joke about salesmen needing big feet— so they can get a foot in the customer's door. They are also supposed to put their best foot forward, and make sure the shoe is shined. You are putting your *whole self* forward

when you apply for a job and you want it to make the best possible impression. That first impression is very important—because sometimes it is the only one you have a chance to make. Maybe you are the greatest fry cook that McDonald's ever interviewed, or the most efficient file clerk a company will ever find. But if you show up for the interview with a two-day beard and dirty fingernails, or frowzy hair and soiled pants suit, you may not get the chance to prove your ability. Writers often complain bitterly that editors don't read far enough into their stories to get to the good part, but editors quickly point out that they don't have to eat the whole egg to know it's bad. A writer must make his beginning the best part of his story. The same thing applies in trying to sell yourself as an employee. So put your best self forward.

Contest rules often note that "neatness doesn't count." Even so, the wise contestant doesn't submit a sloppy entry. If you are interviewing for a job as a bouncer and demonstrate your strength by picking up the interviewer, chair and all, with one hand, you may get the job even though you look like a tramp. But even here, it won't hurt to be neat. Have someone check you out, parents or friends, if possible. If not, at least look long and critically in your mirror before heading for the interview.

It will also pay to be on time, or early, for your appointment. If you are the last cable splicer on earth, and six communication firms are about to close their doors for lack of spliced cables, you can lie in bed until they come to you. If not, be more considerate and respectful of your prospective employer.

There are different kinds of interviews. A "Help Wanted" ad may say to phone someone at a certain number, and that brief call will be your only opportunity to sell yourself and your abilities. Generally, however, there will be a personal confrontation, eyeball-to-eyeball with your prospective boss or a representative. You must pass inspection before you can go on to the next test.

It is wise to arrive a few minutes before the assigned time, and to make your presence known to whoever is minding the store. Don't goof here because the receptionist may be busy, not as efficient as she ought to be, or otherwise inattentive. So be sure that the proper person knows you are Johnny-on-the-spot. Smile, or at least look pleasant. And don't chew bubble gum or twirl a yo-yo—unless the job involves doing those things.

Because the job you are applying for is merely riveting widgets or weeding potatoes on someone's back forty, don't be tempted to ease up on your selling job. If an employer can get a riveter who can also smile and communicate intelligently, or a potato-weeder who can meet people, he may be more likely to consider him—not only for this job but also for advancement. So look your interviewer in the eye, speak plainly, and smile in a friendly way.

Sometimes you yourself are all that is needed. More often there will be documentary evidence that can help your chances: a diploma, and maybe a list of your courses and grades, letters of recommendation, and character references. Sometimes a birth certificate or other evidence of the fact that you are legally and officially alive is required.

Military history may be helpful, along with apprenticeship papers, union card, and even medical records. Check ahead of time and have all such needed items with you. If you have forgotten something, the job may go to someone else by the time you can get home and back.

Often it is necessary to file a written application for a job. This will include your education, in school and out, and any job experience you have. As with everything else having to do with employment seeking, the key is putting your best foot forward. Unless the job you want is one involving penmanship, it will probably be better to type your résumé. This should include the important biographical facts: name, address, and phone, education, experience, test scores if any are applicable, and a list of references for your character and ability. If you are not the world's greatest writer, speller, or typist, seek competent help. Many people earn their living writing job résumés for others. You may want to have yours done by a professional firm but ask for samples of what they have done so you can make sure it is the sort of thing you want and need. If you think you can do as well or better, hop to it. You will save money and time, and you may also produce something with a more personal touch. In fact, some prospective employers may not look with favor on an expensive professionally prepared résumé. Or they may hire the writer instead of you!

There are two sides to employment, of course, and you should be sure that you are going to get a fair return for your effort. This includes not only salary but working conditions, opportunity for advancement, vacations, holidays, insurance, and other benefits. Remember, however, that employers want to hire workers, not instant retirees. If your first question is how soon can you get a pension, the boss may wonder how diligently you will work. And if you don't earn him money, your employer can't afford to pay *you*.

Two additional tips for the interview: Don't go to such an important meeting "cold." Do the necessary homework and be prepared not only to answer questions but to ask them. Know something about the job you are applying for, and the company you hope to be part of. It is also generally recommended that you show interest in a particular job, or job area. Only as a last resort—such as imminent starvation, or a mortgage long past due—should you tell the interviewer, "I'll take anything." That doesn't do justice to either of you.

DOES THIS JOB HAVE A FUTURE?

You probably don't want to sign up for a life of riveting handles onto shovels, or weeding potatoes. If after a certain length of time you can start *selling* shovels or potatoes, managing the office, or designing better products for the factory, your career will look brighter. Investigate these important aspects of the new job you are considering.

Ask your potential employer about the future of the job you are seeking. He will be so much happier with this question than one about retirement that he may predict you will soon rise to the top and sit at a desk in the head office.

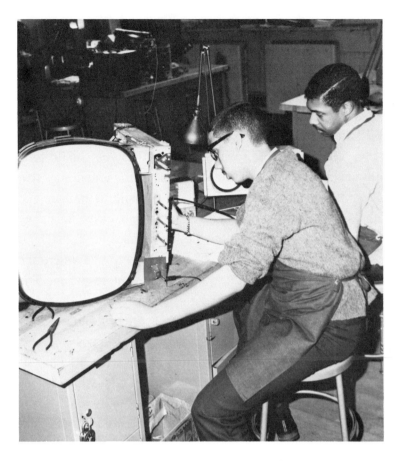

This may or may not be true, and to such rosy promises you should add what other more realistic impressions and observations you can obtain. If possible, talk with people working on the job you are considering. If *all* of them have been riveting shovels for fifteen years with the same kind of hammer, or weeding potatoes on the same forty acres without a letup or a shot at any other part of the operation, your future is probably not as bright as the manager would have you believe. If you investigate a job in a factory with five thousand assemblers working at identical tasks, and learn that there is one opening for foreman every five years, simple arithmetic indicates that opportunity for advancement does not abound.

You should also ask *yourself* some searching questions: Will the job be interesting and challenging? Or does it strike you as dull? If so, chances are that you should look further instead of locking yourself into something that doesn't grab you and probably never will. If hunger and other basic needs must be satisfied at all costs, this may make such a job more palatable, of course.

Home is where the heart is, but it may not be where the jobs are. At least, not the jobs *you* are interested in. The work action is generally in large urban areas, unless you hanker to be a cowpoke, a hermit, or a forest ranger. Fortunately, most of us live in or near large cities and this puts us within reasonable distance of a variety of jobs. If you are a farm boy or girl, or live in a hamlet with a population of twenty-four and only weekly bus service to the county seat, you may have to leave home to find much job choice.

You *could* buy a summer vacation ticket from the bus company and tour the country until you find what you are looking for. You *might* find the needle in a haystack, but you might not. Better do some intelligent long-distance scouting via counselors, the newspapers, employment agencies, and friends and family in other cities.

Relocation is an interesting word. It can mean adventure, new surroundings, new friends and acquaintances. Often it means extra pay for someone willing to move across the state, the country, or even the ocean. Be sure to examine all angles of such a move, however. Does the employer pay all your moving expenses? Will he help you find housing, and how expensive will that housing be? For example, some people take jobs in Washington, D.C., and then find they can't afford to live there, don't like it, or both. Just going to work near home is enough of a shock to the nervous system. Adding to it a move filled with many problems may suddenly make life too complicated. So be cautious in accepting a job distant from home, family, or friends, unless one of your immediate goals is to put as much distance as you can between these others and yourself!

There are other costs to a job, of course. Will you need tools, uniforms, or special clothes? If you don't have a car, can you take a bus or subway, or perhaps join a car pool? How much time will commuting take? In the long run it may pay you to take a job nearer home to save time and money and thus come out ahead.

KEEPING A JOB

After having landed a good job the next consideration is that of keeping it. This of course assumes that you *want* to keep it; that you made a wise first choice and are in something you actually get a kick out of doing.

Let's say you are reasonably sure there is opportunity for getting ahead. Do your job, and a little more, if union rules or other restrictions don't prevent that. Be pleasant, friendly, and helpful. Get involved in available activities—sports, clubs, and social events. If there is a suggestion program, participate in it. Let your employer know that you are eager to make progress. This does *not* mean dropping by his office every night to remind him you have been there a month now and haven't had a single raise. Some companies offer training courses in the plant, or at local schools, paying all or part of the costs for their employees. Here is an excellent way to improve your skills and demonstrate to the company that you are the sort of person they should move ahead in their organization.

Shortsighted people scoff at work responsibilities, or laugh with the guy who manages to beat the company out of a day's work for a day's pay. A few do this and get by with it, but if we all goofed off in such a manner the economic world would come to a creaking halt. To survive, we would have to get it started again and then do a better job next time around. It is also possible that the boss wasn't born yesterday, and knows when he is being taken by lazy employees. He may even appreciate the oddballs who work hard, and help them get ahead.

There is an old saying that before you can lead you must be able to follow. Before you can run the store you have to be able to stock the shelves, wait on customers, and make deliveries. Few people are born corporation presidents or factory superintendents. There are situations where people of lesser ability rise to the top because of politics, family relationships, favoritism, or even blackmail. If you find yourself in such an unfair situation you have several choices: marry the boss's daughter and get yourself appointed president at a tender age; grin and bear it, hoping the boss will wake up as the bad apples make a mess of things; or get out and find a work environment that gives *your* talents a chance to shine.

THIS BUSINESS OF ''JOB SECURITY''

Fear of unemployment plagues many people, and those who have been out of work for long periods especially crave security in their jobs. We all like to eat regularly and to have a nice home and the other comforts of life. The trick is not to let this basic need for security make you lose sight of your need for achievement and fulfillment. Many workers cling desperately to their meal-ticket job through thick and thin, secretly hating the battle for survival (and sometimes the job itself as a result). They survive until retirement, and then leave with the vague knowledge that something has been missing. A prison is perhaps the most secure place to be, but none of us want a prisoner's life.

Perhaps the best lesson to learn is that the strongest security is not a steady paycheck but personal satisfaction, an inner joy in knowing you are doing the thing that is right for you. Your personality is a big factor in the approach you take in your career. A job that delights one person may give another ulcers or a case of screaming boredom which can be escaped only at a great price.

You must be the judge of what is right for you. Don't make the mistake of passing up a good job opportunity just for the sake of security, but don't go overboard the other way either. I have a friend who left the firm we both worked for when a ''golden opportunity'' presented itself.

Since that time he has held half a dozen positions, each stimulating, challenging, and financially rewarding. On returning to the city where he started work, he found that those who had stayed on were now earning about as much as he, and had probably done better financially since their living costs were much lower. Yet, with a contented smile, he told me he would probably continue "chasing rainbows" as long as he could find them. That was his thing.

I FIND THE GREAT THING IN THIS WORLD
IS NOT SO MUCH WHERE WE STAND, AS IN
WHAT DIRECTION WE ARE MOVING.

Oliver Wendell Holmes

And Getting Ahead

Old western movies, some of which are still shown on television, often ended with the hero, his horse, and sometimes his lady friend, riding off into the sunset. We were left to assume that they "lived happily ever afterward," with the future resolved into a blissful vacuum. Don't assume that once you have found a job that suits, you too will just gradually fade away into the twilight of employment. In fact, if you want your working career to be something that makes you look forward to Mondays instead of Fridays, you had better not begin fading at all.

You'll probably settle into your new job for a certain length of time before you feel the need to think about getting ahead. But it is well to give it some thought, even before you land the job. Plans for the future often can best be made today or, better yet, should have been made yesterday.

A fortunate few people start at the top. For them the problem is simply how to stay there; they cannot hope to go any farther up. Instead they often go down, or maybe even off the deep end, from sheer boredom. Some writers, actors, and other professionals have made it big the first time out—and failed at nearly everything thereafter. Perhaps a "less fortunate" beginning, some distance from the top, is not so bad after all. Let's assume you are an average person, with an average job, and talk about how you can improve both yourself and your job.

UPGRADING YOU

Poet Robert Burns is remembered for his lines: "Oh wad some power the giftie gie us to see oursels as others see us!" A performance review does tell you how others see you—in this case the people who decide how important you are to their organization. Sometimes we get unfair reviews; sometimes the evaluation tells more about the reviewer than the person reviewed. But be fair before refusing to believe that you "don't get along with people," "can't follow instructions," or "are uncertain when given added responsibility." It seldom profits a reviewer to lie about an employee; generally this is really the way you look to the person who took the time and trouble to score you.

If necessary, try to improve your personality. Improve your knowledge of your present work, and also learn what will be necessary in that new job you are thinking about. If you can, have your employer help with this continuing education. Take classes after work, at night, or on weekends if necessary. Don't overlook correspondence schools. Often you can proceed faster when the study pace is left up to you, although more discipline is required when there is no teacher present to keep you awake and working.

Just as having a family can tie you more tightly to a job, so can debts. Let's hope that your education included enough math for you to know you can't pay $200 in bills each week if you only take home $150. Your character should also be strong enough to withstand the seductions of salesmen, either in person, by telephone, or on television. Often people are trapped by their bills and can't even think of changing jobs, because this might lose several weeks' pay and put them even further in debt. Instead of getting big debts paid off when a raise comes, the unwise often shrug and go deeper into debt for that new car or whatever else seems so important. Obviously, if you are not a slave to money and to material things, you are in a better position to move to a better job when the spirit speaks to you.

SELF-RENEWAL

John Gardner, former secretary of the Department of Health, Education, and Welfare, and founder of the organization Common Cause, wrote a book called *Self-Renewal*. Read it if you are interested in keeping out of the job rut that many seem to get into. Another help is to sit down from time to time and evaluate your situation. You can do this in your head, or better yet, write it down. Type out a list if that helps you: Are you earning enough money? Are other living conditions as good as you desire? Most importantly, are you *happy?* This doesn't mean going around with a silly smirk on your face, telling yourself that every day in every way, you—and the world—are growing better. You can be carrying a crushing load of work and seldom smile, yet be filled with happiness a smirker couldn't comprehend.

Don't fail to establish goals and guidelines. If you don't know where you are or where you are headed, chances are you are going around in circles, if you are moving at all. First, is your job still the right place for you? After several months or a year, you should begin to have a good idea. Don't confuse personalities with the work itself. Maybe you are still crazy about dogs and cats and other small animals—it is just the vet you work for who bugs you. On the other hand, don't let pleasant co-workers blind you to the fact that you aren't in the right spot for your abilities and interests. If there is a vague, nagging feeling that something is missing, something probably is: the satisfaction that should come if the job is right for you.

There was a time when a person who went to work as a miner or a carpenter didn't leave that job until he died. Indeed it was thought that there was something noble about such dedication to a job. For another thing, there weren't all that many different jobs available. Today we can be more flexible, we can look around and shop around. If after a year the shine is really off that career you thought was for you, start thinking about something else.

It costs time and money to train a person who for some time isn't even earning his or her pay, much less making any money for the company. So it hurts to have that person leave. But it is worse if an employee is working under protest, hating every minute of it. For you hurt not just yourself but others as well by continuing as a misfit in your work.

The great city of Rome was built on the remains of earlier cities. In general, archaeologists find most cities are built on cities which themselves rest on earlier cities below. You can do the same in your getting-ahead process: Build a new career on the foundations of the old, rather than starting from scratch. It is sometimes possible to arrange a transfer to a different kind of work, or a different level of the same kind of work, at your present place of employment. Talk it over at the office or plant. How about an outside job, driving the delivery van, for example? You can use much knowledge you have learned at the order desk and will not need as long a break-in period as a new worker. This is the easiest kind of job switch. Keep in mind that a broad knowledge of a business can be an asset, for people with a view of the whole operation can be useful in top level jobs.

It may turn out, of course, that your only hope for happiness is a complete new start elsewhere, maybe even another city. Be glad you figured this out before you were ready to retire, a bitter person drained by forty years on a job you despised—a job which took everything from you and offered nothing in return except a paycheck.

It is estimated that a person will hold seven jobs on the

average during a lifetime. These may actually be the same job in different locations, but in some cases they may be distinctly different jobs. There is no disgrace here, especially if most of the changes are in an upward direction. Remember, however, that while it is wrong to bury yourself early in the wrong job, it is also wrong to jump from job to job every few months. After a time it becomes dif-

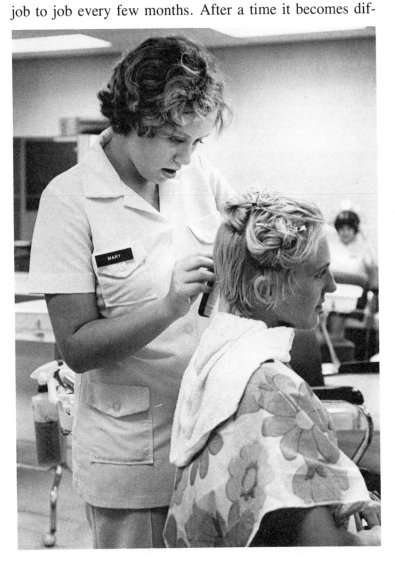

ficult to explain why you need three extra sheets of paper to list your employment history for the last two years. There may be other reasons for changing jobs, of course. Your work may be wiped out by automation, a failing market, curtailment of a government program, environmental considerations, or some other factor beyond your control. You must be prepared to find another job, with or without help from your employer, the Labor Department, or the government.

GOAL TO GO

While many people agree that money isn't everything, they also believe that whatever is in second place is running far behind. Money won't buy happiness, they admit, but neither will happiness buy money. With plenty of the green stuff, the saying goes, nothing else matters all that much. What if it *is* a rat race, you can cry on the way to the bank, can't you?

Recently, however, this view has been seriously challenged by many people, mostly the young. For them, money is secondary to other values, and they are happier doing something that satisfies them than making thirty or forty thousand a year along the ulcer route. It has been pointed out that you can eat only one steak and wear only one suit of clothes at a time. A Volkswagen, or even a Honda, will get you where you are going, and the scenery looks pretty much the same as it does from a Cadillac. The more you earn, the more Uncle Sam demands. So the philosophy of some people is that the greatest happiness is to be content with little.

An oversimplified view is that there are only two types of people: those who work for money, and those who don't. Actually there is a great variety of people who assign varying degrees of importance to material things and to values. How you feel about such matters will determine your lifestyle and your plan for the future. Maybe it is important for you to be earning twice as high a salary within ten years. With inflation puffing up costs, we had all better make that a goal. But perhaps you want to grow in other ways: toward being the finest doctor in the state or the country, the most effective teacher, the most knowledgeable engineer or scientist, the most skillful house painter or auto mechanic.

Successful growth seldom comes of its own accord. If you sit back for the forty years you are destined to work, your experience may well be that of the first year only, repeated dully for thirty-nine more years, each a more blurred carbon copy of the previous one. Chances are that you want your career to stay in sharper focus; that you want to do new things, different things, meaningful things, No one can better take you along those paths than you can take yourself.

ELEVEN

Survival
in the World of Work

In spite of bold promises of a time when work will be a relic of the Dark Ages, more of our people are working than ever before. It can be argued that something is wrong here. Perhaps someday an enlightened society will work less because it demands less, preferring to spend more time in leisure pursuits than earning dollars to pay bills. However, for the near future, most of us will continue to work.

Specifically, you are going to spend as much time gainfully employed as sleeping, and far more time working than playing. How this much work affects you will depend on the sort of person you are. But however you feel about it, it seems sensible to work at something that is most meaningful and rewarding to you.

There are two approaches to work. One is just to drift into something, trusting to luck or Divine Providence that it will work out. So you blunder into the first thing available and then go through life in a pained daze from Monday to Friday. If your philosophy considers work as a prison sentence, about the best you can hope for is to get through it alive and then to enjoy a brief rest before passing on. "It's a living" is a common expression used to justify a dull job. Such employment keeps us off the streets, and the wolf away from the door. If this is the best you can do, so be it. But you should be able to do much more.

The better approach, of course, is the one we have been talking about all through this book—choose a job you are suited to. Years ago this was a hard thing to do, for often there were few jobs available and these in very little variety. Today the reverse situation prevails, and the problem can be tough because there is so *much* choice! I have just looked at Sunday's "Help Wanted" ads in the Phoenix, Arizona, paper. There are eight pages of jobs advertised, ranging from upholsterer to seamstress to company president aide, from tool-room attendant to agricultural engineer. With 30,000 job classifications to choose from there has to be something that, if not exciting, is at least less of a chore than other jobs. If you will spend more time now in intelligent job planning, you will spend a lot less of the next four decades complaining about your life. The English philosopher R. G. Collingwood gives a hint of the well-being that goes with finding one's right place in the work world:

> There is no truer and more abiding happiness than the knowledge that one is free to go on doing, day by day, the best work one can do, in the kind one likes best, and that this work is absorbed by a steady market and thus supports one's own life. Perfect freedom is reserved for the man who lives by his own work and in that work does what he wants to do.

May *you* find this abiding happiness and perfect freedom!

For Further Reading

Anderson, B. D. *Introduction to College.* New York: Holt, Rinehart and Winston, Inc., 1969.

Arnold, Arnold. *Career Choices for the Seventies.* New York: Macmillan, Inc., 1971.

Belman, Harry S., and **Shertzer, Bruce.** *My Career Guidebook.* St. Paul, Minn.: Bruce Publishing Company, 1967.

Berg, Ivar. *Education and Jobs: The Great Training Robbery.* Boston: Beacon Press, 1971.

Berger, Peter. *The Human Shape of Work.* Chicago: Henry Regnery Company, 1973.

Best, Fred, ed. *The Future of Work.* New York: Prentice-Hall, Inc., 1973.

Borow, Henry. *Man in a World at Work.* Boston: Houghton Mifflin Company, 1964.

Brown, Newell. *After College, What: A Career Exploration Handbook.* New York: Grosset & Dunlap, Inc., 1971.

Butler, E. A. *How to Move In and Move Up.* New York: Macmillan, Inc., 1970.

Casewit, Curtis W. *How to Get a Job Overseas.* New York: Arco Publishing Co., Inc., 1970.

De Grazia, Sebastian. *Of Time, Work and Leisure.* New York: Anchor Press, 1962.

Duckat, Walter. *Guide to Professional Careers.* New York: Julian Messner, 1970.

Fanning, J. *Working When You Want to Work.* New York: Macmillan, Inc., 1969.

Farnsworth, Marjorie. *The Young Woman's Guide to an Academic Career.* New York: Richards Rosen Press, Inc., 1974.

Ferrari, Erma P. *Careers for You.* Nashville, Tenn.: Abingdon Press, 1969.

Friedman, Sande, and **Schwartz, Lois.** *No Experience Necessary.* New York: Dell Publishing Co., Inc., 1971.

Gardner, John W. *Excellence.* New York: Harper & Row, Publishers, 1961.

————. *Self-Renewal.* New York: Harper & Row, Publishers, 1964.

Gibson, Mary B. *The Family Circle Book of Careers at Home.* New York: Popular Library, 1972.

Green, Thomas F. *Work, Leisure and the American Schools.* New York: Random House, Inc., 1968.

Harter, Walter. *Your Career in Unusual Occupations.* New York: David McKay Co., Inc., 1971.

Hopke, William E., ed. *The Encyclopedia of Careers and Vocational Guidance. Vols. I & II* (Revised Edition). Chicago: J. C. Ferguson Publishing Co., 1972.

Irish, Richard K. *Go Hire Yourself an Employer.* New York: Anchor Press, 1973.

Joseph, James. *Two Hundred Fifty Careers Out of Doors.* Chicago: Henry Regnery Company, 1973.

Keefe, John, and **Stein, Stanley J.** *The Joy of Work.* New York: Richards Rosen Press, Inc., 1974.

Kelly Services Staff. *The Kelly Girl Second Career Guide.* Boston: Little, Brown and Company, 1973.

Levitan, Sar A., and **Johnston, William B.** *Work Is Here to Stay, Alas.* Salt Lake City, Utah: Olympus Publishing Co., 1973.

Liston, Robert A. *On the Job Training and Where to Get It.* New York: Julian Messner, 1973.

McClure, Larry, and **Buan, Carolyn.** *Essays on Career Education.* Washington, D.C.: Government Printing Office, 1973.

McGrath, Lee, and **Scobey, Jean.** *Creative Careers for Women.* New York: Essandess Special Editions, 1968.

Rhodes, James A. *Vocational Education and Guidance.* Columbus, Ohio: Charles E. Merrill Publishing Company, 1970.

──────. *Alternative to a Decadent Society.* Indianapolis, Indiana: Howard W. Sams & Co., 1969.

Secretary, Health, Education and Welfare. *Work In America.* Cambridge, Mass.: The M.I.T. Press, 1973.

Shertzer, Bruce. *Career Exploration and Planning.* Boston: Houghton Mifflin Company, 1973.

Splaver, Sarah. *Non-Traditional Careers for Women.* New York: Julian Messner, 1973.

Venables, E. *Leaving School and Starting Work.* New York: Pergamon Press, Inc., 1968.

Wurman, Richard Saul. *Yellow Pages of Learning Resources.* Cambridge, Mass.: The M.I.T. Press, 1972.

You and Your Job: What Is It? Where Is It? How to Get It. How to Keep It. Where Do You Go From Here? Chicago: J. C. Ferguson Publishing Co., 1969.

About the Author

D. S. HALACY, JR., well-known for his many outstanding books for young readers, was born in Charleston, South Carolina, and graduated from Arizona State University with a B.A. in English. He has served two terms as an Arizona State Senator, during which time he chaired the Education Committee and helped initiate Arizona's pioneering Career Education program.

Mr. Halacy now lives in Glendale, Arizona, with his wife and family. He counts among his special interests a love of flying his sailplane.